text and
photographs by
Jill Dupleix

whitecap

Jill Dupleix
very
simple
food

notes

All measurements are given
in standard U.S. cups and
spoons. All eggs are free-
range and extra large; all
herbs are fresh; all salt is
sea salt, and all pepper is
freshly ground black pepper
unless otherwise stated.
All recipe ideas serve 4
unless otherwise suggested.

Creative Director Mary Evans
Project Editors Janet Illsley and
Norma MacMillan
Production Phil Dauncey

First published in 2003 by
Quadrille Publishing Limited
Alhambra House
27-31 Charing Cross Road
London WC2H OLS

First published in the United States
and Canada in 2003 by Whitecap Books
For more information, contact
Whitecap Books, 351 Lynn Avenue,
North Vancouver, British Columbia,
Canada V7J 2C4

Text and photographs
© 2003 Jill Dupleix
Design and layout
© 2003 Quadrille Publishing Limited

The rights of the author have
been asserted.

Cataloguing in Publication Data:
a catalogue record for this book is
available from the British Library.

ISBN 1-55285-532-5
Printed in China

www.jilldupleix.com

This book is all about everyday food—simple food that uses smart tricks. It's full of ideas for that chicken breast, fish fillet, or bag of potatoes you just brought home. I've designed it to give you the food you need to survive the working week, and the food you love to share with friends on the weekend.

I like flavors that taste fresh and bright, recipes that don't make you nervous, and food that is healthy enough to keep us out of the clutches of diet fads and self-help gurus. But the real secret to very simple food is very good produce. Shop well, and you will cook well.

I also think it's time to rethink some of the conventions of the day. Why must a "proper" meal be made up of three courses, instead of a tableful of small and interesting dishes ready to share? If we really love cheese or salad, why don't we make them the heart of the meal rather than something to get through before we can enjoy the entrée? Why don't we picnic inside, and take our dining table outdoors? I have no idea why not.

I don't make my own pastry, refuse to deep-fry, won't pit olives, and will never be found peeling grapes. I also believe it's perfectly acceptable to cheat at cooking as long as you don't kill anyone.

The trick is to keep things simple, for ourselves and our food. Very simple.

Jill

starters

Cucumber "sandwiches"

This is a blindingly simple and endlessly flexible idea for all you canapé crusaders out there. Cucumber rounds give you freshness and crunch, and carry all manner of sympathetic flavors, such as smoked salmon (featured here), smoked trout, fresh shrimp, or crab.

Peel the cucumber lengthwise, leaving a few thin strips of skin for a decorative effect. Cut the cucumber into $\frac{1}{2}$-inch slices—you should get around 32 slices.

Arrange half the cucumber slices on a board. Dab a little horseradish sauce on each one to help the salmon stay in place. Cut the smoked salmon into 16 pieces, fold loosely, and arrange on top of the cucumber slices on the board. Season with salt and pepper.

Cover each with another cucumber slice. Add a little dab of horseradish sauce and top with a parsley leaf and a salted caper, then serve.

MAKES 16
1 hothouse cucumber
2 tbsp horseradish sauce
5 oz thinly sliced smoked
    salmon
sea salt
freshly ground black pepper
16 flat-leaf parsley sprigs
16 salted capers

Lemon mussels

Why serve mussels out of their shells when the shells can double as perfect little appetizer plates? Do this as a big party platter, or as elegant individual first courses.

Discard any broken mussels, and those that do not close when sharply tapped. Scrub the mussels well and pull out any little "beards." Put the wine, parsley stems, and garlic in a large pot and bring to a boil. Add the mussels, cover with the lid, and cook for 1 minute, then shake the pan, remove the lid, and take out the mussels that are open. Repeat this process, then discard any mussels that haven't opened.

Let the mussels cool to room temperature, then discard the top half-shells, saving four. Arrange the mussels on platters. Mix the preserved lemon with the minced parsley, olive oil, and lemon juice. Spoon a little lemony dressing onto each mussel in the half-shell.

Beat the mayonnaise with the paprika and spoon into the reserved shells for dipping. Put one on each platter and serve.

SERVES 4
3 lb fresh mussels
1 cup dry white wine
handful of parsley stems
2 garlic cloves, squashed
2 tbsp minced preserved lemon
2 tbsp minced parsley
2 tbsp extra virgin olive oil
1 tbsp lemon juice
2 tbsp good mayonnaise
$\frac{1}{2}$ tsp paprika

soy-roasted nuts

Soy-roasted nuts

This simple technique not only freshens up mixed nuts, it coats them with a lightly crunchy, seductively sweet-salty flavor. Tamari is a wheat-free soy sauce, available in Asian markets and helpful supermarkets.

Heat the oven to 350°F. Line the bottom of a shallow roasting pan or baking sheet with foil and scatter the nuts on the foil. Roast for 10 minutes, tossing the nuts occasionally.

Mix the tamari or soy sauce and sugar in a bowl. Remove the pan from the oven and tip the nuts into the bowl, tossing until well coated. Using a slotted spoon, return the nuts to the foil-lined pan. Roast for up to 10 minutes until they are dry, tossing every minute or so and watching carefully to be sure they don't burn.

Leave the roasted nuts in the pan until they are completely cool, then store in an airtight jar until needed. Serve with drinks, or scattered through salads.

MAKES 1 lb
1 lb mixed shelled nuts
   (eg blanched almonds,
   brazil nuts, hazelnuts,
   pistachios)
½ cup tamari or soy sauce
1 tbsp sugar

Smoked salmon martini

Save on making cocktail snacks for your next party, by putting the cocktail snack in the cocktail. First, you sip the vodka martini, then you eat the vodka-marinated smoked salmon and the olive. Then you have another one.

First, chill four martini glasses until they are frosty. Cut the smoked salmon slices in half lengthwise, twist each piece into a spiral, and place in the glasses.

Pour the vodka and dry vermouth over ice into a shaker, stir well, and strain into the glasses. Add an olive to each glass and serve.

MAKES 4
2 thin slices smoked salmon
1 $\frac{1}{4}$ cups vodka
$\frac{1}{4}$ cup dry vermouth
4 green or stuffed olives

Parmesan crackers

These rich, cheesy little crackers make the perfect nibble with drinks. Send out a stack with a tray of icy cold dry martinis or tall, frosty glasses of chilled white wine, or serve them with little cups of creamy vegetable soup.

Heat the oven to 350°F. Cut the butter into small dice. Put the butter, flour, cheese, sea salt, pepper, and cayenne in the food processor and whiz until sandy. Add the ice water and whiz again until the dough is moist and clumpy. Add extra water if necessary.

Form into a ball, then roll out to ½-inch thickness on a lightly floured surface and cut into 2-inch rounds. Place on a nonstick baking sheet, brush lightly with beaten egg, and scatter the thyme and rosemary over the tops.

Bake for 10 to 12 minutes or until lightly golden, then transfer to a wire rack to cool. Store in an airtight container for up to 2 weeks.

MAKES 12

7 tbsp (3½oz) butter, chilled

1 cup all-purpose flour

¾ cup grated parmesan, cheddar, or gruyère

½ tsp sea salt

freshly ground black pepper

pinch of cayenne pepper

1 tbsp ice water

1 free-range egg, beaten

1 tbsp thyme and rosemary leaves

Thai corn cakes

Crisp, golden little fritters that practically pop in the mouth with juicy corn kernels. Stack high and drizzle with sweet, seedy Thai chili sauce.

Whiz half the corn in a blender to a purée. Pound the garlic, shallots, and cilantro stems until smashed. Add to the blender with the sugar, fish sauce, salt, and pepper, and whiz to a purée.

Add the flour and whiz for 1 minute, then add the eggs and process for another 30 seconds. Tip into a bowl and fold through the remaining corn, reserving 1 tbsp for serving.

Heat the oil in a heavy frying pan until it starts to smoke. Drop 4 tablespoons of batter into the pan, spacing them apart, and cook until golden, turning once. Remove and drain on paper towels. Keep warm while you make the remaining cakes.

Scatter with corn kernels and green onions, and drizzle with sweet chili sauce to serve.

MAKES 16

2 cups drained canned corn kernels

2 garlic cloves, peeled

2 shallots, peeled

2 cilantro stems

1 tsp sugar

1 tbsp Thai fish sauce

1 tsp sea salt

1/2 tsp freshly ground black pepper

2/3 cup all-purpose flour

2 extra large free-range eggs

2 tbsp vegetable oil, for frying

2 green onions, minced

1/2 cup Asian sweet chili sauce

party sushi

Party sushi

Make these just before guests arrive and keep, tightly covered, in the refrigerator, or turn the making of them into a party piece, and keep them rolling out to order. Party, or "temaki," sushi are light, fresh, and healthy, and fun to eat in your hands. Add cooked shrimp, sashimi-quality tuna, or avocado, if you wish.

MAKES 20
Sushi rice:
¼ cup rice vinegar
2 tbsp sugar
1 tsp salt
2 cups sushi rice
2 cups water

To assemble:
½ hothouse cucumber
1 red bell pepper
1 yellow bell pepper
2 tsp wasabi powder
1 tbsp good mayonnaise
20 sheets nori (toasted seaweed sheet)
8 oz thinly sliced smoked salmon

To make the sushi rice dressing, gently heat the rice vinegar, sugar, and salt in a small pan until the sugar has dissolved, then cool.

Rinse the rice in a strainer under cold running water. Drain well, then tip into a saucepan and add the water. Bring to a boil, cover tightly, and simmer very gently for 15 minutes. Remove from the heat and leave for 10 minutes undisturbed, then tip the rice out onto a baking sheet.

Sprinkle the rice with the cooled dressing, tossing it well with a wooden spoon to cool it quickly. Keep the rice covered with a damp cloth until ready to use, which should be the same day.

Cut the cucumber and bell peppers into thin batons or strips, discarding the pepper core and seeds. Mix the wasabi powder to a paste with the mayonnaise.

Place a heaped tablespoon of sushi rice on the lefthand side of a sheet of nori. Add a dab of wasabi mayonnaise, a small fold of smoked salmon, some cucumber, and red and yellow pepper strips, and roll from left to right into a cone shape. A few grains of rice will help the final flap to stick. Eat in the hands.

Tuna with sesame soy

Really fresh tuna has a pure, sweet flavor and melt-in-the-mouth texture. This no-cook, no-fuss first course makes the most of tuna by teaming it with soy sauce, sesame oil, and mirin (sweet rice wine), available from Japanese food stores and helpful supermarkets.

Trim the tuna of all bloodlines and cut into a neat shape to enable you to cut it into small dice, around ½ inch. Discard any obvious sinews or icky bits.

Whisk the soy sauce, mirin, sesame oil, and mustard together in a bowl. Add the tuna and toss lightly to coat in the dressing.

Mix the rice vinegar and olive oil with sea salt and pepper in a second bowl. Add the watercress and toss in the dressing, then arrange on four serving plates.

Pile the tuna in little pyramids on top of the leaves, and scatter with the chives. Serve with chopsticks.

SERVES 4
12oz fresh sashimi-quality
tuna
1 tbsp soy sauce
1 tbsp mirin
1 tsp toasted sesame oil
½ tsp Dijon mustard
1 tsp rice vinegar
1 tbsp olive oil
sea salt
freshly ground black pepper
1 cup watercress leaves
1 tbsp minced chives

Smoked salmon rolls

These glamorous rolls fulfill my three main criteria for easy entertaining: they take only minutes to make; they can be done ahead of time; and they look like a million dollars. Serve as a sit-down first course, or with drinks.

Beat 1 tbsp horseradish into the mascarpone or crème fraîche. Gradually add the rest to taste, until the mixture is hot enough for you. Add the chives, sea salt, and pepper, and fold them through the cream. (You can make this beforehand and refrigerate it.)

Trim the smoked salmon into 8 strips, each 2 x 6 inches. Place a spoonful of the horseradish cream on one end of each strip and roll up. It doesn't matter if the edges are a bit ragged.

Sit each smoked salmon roll on its end, and scatter extra chives on the exposed cream at the top. (You can even do this an hour or two beforehand and refrigerate until required.) Serve one or two salmon rolls per person.

MAKES 8

2 tbsp hot horseradish sauce

2 cups mascarpone or crème fraîche

2 tbsp minced chives, plus extra to serve

sea salt

freshly ground black pepper

8 oz thinly sliced smoked salmon

Salami tarts

I had some leftover pastry and salami, so I did the only thing possible—I made salami tarts, chilled a bottle of Spanish sherry, and invited people over for a drink. The softer and fresher the salami—look for a Venetian-style "soppressa" —the better the tart.

Heat the oven to 400°F. Roll out the pastry thinly. Remove the skin from the salami slices. Place one salami slice on the pastry and cut around it, leaving a ½-inch border of pastry. Use this as your size guide for cutting out 10 identical pastry rounds.

Brush each pastry round with beaten egg and top with a slice of salami. Bake for 10 minutes or until the pastry borders are puffy and golden. Transfer to a wire rack—they will crisp as they cool.

To cook the Swiss chard, wash it well and place in a saucepan with just the water clinging to the leaves. Cover and cook over high heat, tossing occasionally, until the leaves wilt and the juices evaporate. Let cool, then squeeze out excess water. Toss in the olive oil, with sea salt and lots of pepper.

Serve the salami tarts at room temperature, topped with a little mound of wilted Swiss chard.

MAKES 10
1 lb ready-rolled frozen
puff pastry, thawed
12 slices salami, around
2½-inch diameter
1 free-range egg, beaten
7 oz Swiss chard leaves
1 tbsp extra virgin olive oil
sea salt
freshly ground black pepper

prosciutto grissini

salads

Carrot and orange salad

A crisp, refreshing salad, this glows with warm, sweet spices and almost fluorescent sunny colors. It's perfect for a warm day, when you can scatter sliced summer radishes over the top. It's also perfect for a cold day, when it brings sunshine and the bite of winter's oranges to a meal of grilled fish, chicken, or lamb.

SERVES 6

1 lb carrots

1 orange

handful of cilantro and mint
    leaves

Dressing:

2 tbsp orange juice

1 tbsp lemon juice

2 tbsp extra virgin olive oil

sea salt

freshly ground black pepper

$1/2$ tsp ground cumin

$1/2$ tsp ground cinnamon

1 tsp confectioners' sugar

Peel the carrots and grate them coarsely. Peel the orange with a knife, removing all white pith. Cut it crosswise into $1/2$-inch-thick slices, then into small segments.

Whisk the dressing ingredients together in a large bowl. Add the grated carrot, orange segments, and cilantro and mint leaves. Toss lightly to serve.

Bacon and tomato salad

This could be too simple for some, but I love putting fresh salads centerstage and making a meal of them. That way, I can eat my favorite foods, such as crisp bacon, without going overboard on them. Turn this salad into a meal with some pan-fried haloumi cheese, chicken livers, or one of Terry's fried eggs (page 136).

To make the dressing, combine the olive oil, vinegar, mustard, sea salt, and pepper in a large bowl, and whisk well until combined. Cut half of the cherry tomatoes in half and marinate in the dressing.

Cook the bacon under a preheated broiler until crisp. Drain on paper towels and break or cut into thick batons.

Wash and spin the salad leaves dry, then toss in the dressing with the marinated tomatoes and the whole tomatoes. Add the bacon and toss lightly, then distribute among four dinner plates and serve.

SERVES 4
8oz cherry tomatoes
4 thick bacon slices
8oz arugula or other
salad leaves

Dressing:
2 tbsp extra virgin olive oil
1 tbsp red wine vinegar
1 tsp Dijon mustard
sea salt
freshly ground black pepper

feta-tomato salad

Feta-tomato salad

Turn a block of creamy feta cheese into food for the gods with a Greek chorus of chili, olives, herbs, and good olive oil. Serve with drinks, scatter over salads, take on picnics, or serve as part of a lazy al fresco lunch with lots of crusty bread.

Finely slice the chili into rings and place in a bowl with the olives, rosemary, and oregano. Add the olive oil and pepper, and stir to combine. (You won't need salt, as feta is quite salty.)

Rinse the feta, pat dry, and place in a dish. Pour the marinade on top, cover, and leave overnight, or at least for a few hours.

Lift the feta out of the marinade and arrange on a serving plate in its original blocks, or cut into bite-sized cubes. Cut the tomatoes in half and add to the marinade to coat lightly, then spoon over the feta. Serve with crusty bread.

SERVES 4 TO 6
1 small, hot red chili pepper
2 tbsp kalamata olives
5 rosemary sprigs
1 tsp dried oregano
$\frac{1}{2}$ cup extra virgin olive oil
freshly ground black pepper
14 oz good feta cheese
8 oz cherry or baby roma
   tomatoes

Warm spring salad

A fresh, light, warm salad that fills the kitchen with spring-like aromas. Use fresh peas and fava beans in season, or frozen ones out of season—they're perfectly acceptable.

Cook the potatoes in simmering salted water for about 15 minutes until tender. Cook the peas, fava beans, and green beans in a separate pan of simmering salted water (with the shallots to make peeling easier) until tender, about 5 minutes. Drain, refresh in cold water, and set aside. Pick out the shallots, peel, and finely slice.

Heat half the olive oil in a frying pan and gently cook the shallots for 2 minutes. Add the peas and beans, and toss to heat through. Drain the potatoes, cut in half on the diagonal, and add to the pan. Remove from the heat, add the remaining olive oil, the vinegar, salt, and pepper, and toss well.

Scatter the arugula on four warmed plates and top with the beans, peas, and potatoes. Drizzle any remaining dressing over and serve.

SERVES 4
12 waxy boiling potatoes
(eg Yukon gold)
sea salt
1 lb fresh green peas, shelled
1 lb fresh fava beans,
shelled
8 oz fine green beans,
trimmed
3 shallots
3 tbsp extra virgin olive oil
2 tbsp red wine vinegar
freshly ground black pepper
5 oz baby arugula leaves or
watercress

Warm lentil salad

The great thing about these lentils and their pushy little tomato and mint dressing is that they go with anything. Serve them as a salad, as a meal with a fried egg on top, or with roast chicken. The best lentils are the slate-green French "lentilles de Puy," available from good food stores.

Rinse the lentils and place in a saucepan with the onion, garlic, bay leaves, and 4 cups cold water. Bring to a boil, then reduce the heat and simmer gently for 20 minutes or until the lentils are just tender. Drain thoroughly.

To make the dressing, cut the tomatoes in half, discard the juice and seeds, then chop the flesh. In a bowl, combine the chopped tomato with the mint, parsley, sea salt, pepper, extra virgin olive oil, and red wine vinegar.

Toss the still warm drained lentils in the tomato dressing, and divide among four salad plates. Serve warm.

SERVES 4

1$\frac{1}{3}$ cups green or brown
  lentils
1 onion, minced
2 garlic cloves, smashed
2 bay leaves

Dressing:
2 tomatoes
2 tbsp chopped mint
1 tbsp roughly chopped
  flat-leaf parsley
sea salt
freshly ground black pepper
2 tbsp extra virgin olive oil
1 tbsp red wine vinegar

Torn mozzarella and peppers

I fell in love with this torn salad at Geoff Lindsay's opalescent Pearl restaurant in Melbourne, Australia. It looks like a bottomless pizza, and should be served with crusty bread or warmed flat bread. Fresh buffalo milk mozzarella is heavenly. If you can't find it, you could use good feta or fresh ricotta.

Holding the peppers upright, cut the "sides" away from the core and seeds, then cut each piece into $\frac{1}{2}$-inch squares.

Combine the peppers with the olive oil, sea salt, and pepper in a saucepan and stew gently over a low heat for 10 to 15 minutes, without allowing them to "fry" or brown. Remove from the heat and let cool until barely warm.

To serve, set out four dinner plates or one very large platter. Using a slotted spoon, arrange the peppers over the plate, saving the oil. Tear the parsley leaves into shreds with your fingers and scatter over the top.

Drain the mozzarella and pat dry. Tear the soft, fresh cheese into small bits with your fingers, discarding any thick skin, and dot around the plate at random. Drizzle with the reserved oil to serve.

SERVES 4
2 red bell peppers
2 yellow bell peppers
2 tbsp extra virgin olive oil
sea salt
freshly ground black pepper
2 flat-leaf parsley sprigs
2 fresh mozzarella bocconcini
(balls), each about 4 oz

Spanish café salad

Every country with a café culture does a great café salad—a casual combination of readily available produce. This is my idea of a Spanish café salad, using Spain's beautiful serrano ham. It's extremely flexible—you could use prosciutto instead, or add some fresh goat cheese, or leave out the artichoke hearts, to make it your own.

SERVES 4

5oz fine green beans, trimmed

8oz asparagus, trimmed

salt

2 tomatoes

½ hothouse cucumber

8oz mixed salad leaves (eg baby romaine lettuce, arugula, curly endive)

8 small artichoke hearts, preserved in oil

2 tbsp olives

12 thin slices serrano ham

Dressing:

2 tbsp extra virgin olive oil

1 tbsp sherry or red wine vinegar

sea salt

freshly ground black pepper

Cook the green beans and asparagus in simmering salted water for 4 minutes. Drain and cool under cold running water, then drain again.

Cut the tomatoes into quarters, or eighths if large. Peel the cucumber, halve lengthwise, and slice finely.

To make the dressing, whisk the ingredients together in a large bowl. Toss the leaves, green beans, and asparagus in the dressing and arrange on four dinner plates. Toss the tomatoes, cucumber, artichoke hearts, and olives in any remaining dressing and scatter them freely over the leaves.

Using a fork, pull a few of the buried leaves to the surface. Drape the slices of serrano ham on top of the salad and serve.

japanese salmon with mirin

Japanese salmon with mirin

A light, fresh, tangy salad that's as cool as a cucumber on a warm summer's day or evening. If you think there are too many combinations of salmon and cucumber in this book, you're probably right, but I find the two irresistible.

Score the skin of the cucumber lengthwise with the tines of a fork, then slice finely. Combine the lime or lemon juice, rice vinegar, mirin, sea salt, pepper, sugar, and chives in a bowl, and stir until the sugar has dissolved. Add the cucumber slices, toss to coat, and set aside until ready to serve.

SERVES 4
1 hothouse cucumber
1 tbsp lime or lemon juice
1 tbsp rice vinegar
1 tbsp mirin (Japanese rice wine)
sea salt
freshly ground black pepper
1 tsp sugar
2 tbsp minced chives
1 tbsp vegetable oil
1 lb fresh salmon fillet
2 tbsp olive oil

Heat the oil in a nonstick frying pan and sear the salmon fillet on both sides until almost cooked through, but still pink in the center. Let cool, then divide into bite-sized flakes with your fingers.

Drain the cucumber slices, reserving the liquid. Arrange in small mounds on four dinner plates and top with the flaked salmon. Whisk the olive oil with 2 tbsp of the cucumber dressing, plus salt and pepper, and spoon over and around the salmon.

Chicken Waldorf

The real reason I lightened up the famous salad of apple, celery, and walnuts from The Waldorf Astoria in New York is so I can eat more of it. Do this when you have a crowd to feed for Sunday lunch.

Rinse the chicken and place in a wide, shallow pan. Cover with cold water, add the bay leaf and onion half, and bring to just below the boil. Skim off any froth, and simmer gently for 15 minutes. Then cover, remove from the heat, and let steep for 30 minutes. Drain and cool. (You can prepare to this point in advance, although the chicken will be nicer if it isn't refrigerated.)

To make the dressing, whisk the mayonnaise, yogurt, apple juice, lemon juice, salt, and pepper together in a bowl.

Lightly toast the walnuts in a hot, dry pan for a couple of minutes. Remove any strings from the celery, then finely slice. Quarter and core the apples, then dice finely. Add to the dressing with the celery, walnuts, and dill, and toss well.

Finely slice the chicken, add to the salad, and toss lightly. Arrange the lettuce leaves on eight dinner plates or one large buffet plate, and spoon the salad on top.

SERVES 8
4 chicken breast halves
1 bay leaf
$\frac{1}{2}$ onion
2 tbsp roughly chopped walnuts
4 celery stalks
2 red or green apples
2 tbsp minced fresh dill
crisp lettuce leaves, to serve

Dressing:
1 tbsp good mayonnaise
1 tbsp plain yogurt
2 tbsp apple juice
1 tsp lemon juice
sea salt
freshly ground black pepper

Fig and radicchio salad

When figs are in season, I keep trying to find new ways of eating them so that I can fit more in. This salad combines the rich, warm colors of ripe purple figs, pink prosciutto, and ruby-toned radicchio leaves with the crunch of fennel and freshness of mint.

Separate the radicchio leaves, then tear each one roughly in two or three. Very finely slice the fennel bulb crosswise. Quarter the figs.

In a large bowl, whisk the dressing ingredients together. Lightly toss the radicchio leaves, sliced fennel, and mint leaves in the dressing, then arrange on four dinner plates.

Arrange the figs on top, and tuck in the slices of prosciutto. Roughly chop or pinch the cheese into sections and scatter over the top. Drizzle any remaining dressing over the salad and serve, with Italian grissini (breadsticks) or crusty bread.

SERVES 4

2 heads radicchio, trimmed

1 fennel bulb, trimmed

4 ripe figs

20 mint leaves

8 thin slices prosciutto

5oz fresh ricotta or goat
  cheese (about ^{2}/3 cup)

Dressing:

2 tbsp extra virgin olive oil

1 tbsp balsamic vinegar

1 tsp cold water

sea salt

freshly ground black pepper

Pita pockets

This is my very simple version of an Italian snack made with piadina, a soft, unleavened bread from Emiglia-Romana. I use Greek pita bread instead, stuffing it with prosciutto, arugula, and mozzarella, then warming it until the cheese goes gooey.

Heat the oven to 350°F. Toss the arugula leaves in the olive oil with salt and pepper. Drain the mozzarella and slice thinly. Cut the sun-dried tomatoes in half.

Cut or tear the pita breads in half and gently work them open to form pockets. Stuff each pocket with arugula leaves, prosciutto, sun-dried tomatoes, and mozzarella, until quite full. If the bread splits at the side, just wrap in foil to keep it together.

Place the stuffed pitas on a baking sheet and heat through in the oven for 4 to 5 minutes, or until the cheese melts. (Or you can warm them on a medium-hot grill or griddle for just a few minutes, turning once, until the cheese melts.) Don't heat them for too long, or the bread will turn brittle.

Drizzle a generous teaspoonful of pesto into each stuffed pita and serve two halves to each person.

MAKES 4

4 oz arugula leaves

1 tbsp extra virgin olive oil

sea salt

freshly ground black pepper

2 fresh mozzarella bocconcini (balls), each about 4 oz

4 sun-dried tomatoes in oil

4 pita breads

8 slices prosciutto

2 tbsp pesto

Greek stack

A new angle on everyone's favorite Greek salad—serve it stacked high on warm pita bread. If you want something meatier for lunch, add some spiced grilled lamb or a few garlicky sausages to the side.

Discard the outer romaine leaves, then cut the head across into 4 thick, chunky rounds. Thickly slice the tomatoes and season with sea salt and pepper. Cut the feta into 4 chunky slices. Halve the anchovy fillets lengthwise.

To make the dressing, whisk the extra virgin olive oil, lemon juice, sea salt, and pepper in a bowl. Add the olives and toss to coat.

Gently warm the pita bread in a warm oven or under the broiler, and place on four warmed dinner plates. Top each pita with a layer of tomatoes, then a round of lettuce, followed by the feta, another slice of tomato, and a few onion rings. Top with anchovy strips, and spoon the dressing and olives over the whole.

SERVES 4

1 head romaine lettuce
4 ripe tomatoes
sea salt
freshly ground black pepper
14 oz good feta cheese
4 anchovy fillets
3 tbsp extra virgin olive oil
1 tbsp lemon juice
2 tbsp kalamata or small
black olives
4 small pita breads
1 onion, very finely sliced

baked scotch eggs

Salmon and egg tarts

This is a sequel to the little ham and egg pies that appeared in *Simple Food*. Muffin cups are filled with fresh salmon, cream, curry powder, and a whole egg, and baked to produce effortless, pastryless tarts.

Heat the oven to 325°F. Lightly oil or butter a 12-hole muffin pan. Finely chop the raw or cooked salmon and place in a bowl. Add the cream, curry powder, sea salt, pepper, and dill or chives, and mix lightly with a fork.

Divide the salmon mixture among the muffin cups, then break an egg into each one. Using a fork, jiggle the egg white so that it mixes with some of the salmon, keeping the yolk whole.

Bake for 20 to 25 minutes until set. Let cool for 5 minutes, then run a knife around each tart to loosen it and remove to a wire rack.

Scatter with dill or chives and eat warm or at room temperature. Serve one as an appetizer with drinks, two with a salad for lunch, or take them all on a picnic.

MAKES 12

1 tsp olive oil or butter

1 lb salmon fillet, raw or cooked

2 tbsp light cream

1 tsp curry powder

1/2 tsp sea salt

freshly ground black pepper

2 tbsp minced dill or chives, plus extra to serve

12 free-range eggs

Baked Scotch eggs

Because I don't deep-fry, I've invented other ways of having my favorite foods. These Scotch eggs are baked in a muffin pan, in a wrap of bacon. No crumbing, no deep-frying. Simple, really.

Heat the oven to 375°F. Lightly oil a 12-hole muffin pan. Put the eggs in a large pan of hot water, bring to a boil, and simmer for 5 minutes (time from the moment the water starts to bubble). Drain and run cold water over to stop further cooking; cool and peel.

Soak the bread in the milk for 1 minute. Drain and squeeze dry. Combine the bread and sausage in a bowl, using your hands. Add the beaten egg, parsley, nutmeg, salt, and pepper, and mix well.

Line each muffin cup with a bacon slice. Press some sausage into the bottom. Add a boiled egg, pointy end up, and pack the sausage around and over the egg to cover completely. Bake for 20 minutes until nicely browned. Leave in the pan for 10 minutes. Drain off any juices, run a knife around to loosen, and serve hot, warm, or cold.

MAKES 12

1 tsp olive oil

12 extra large free-range eggs

5 slices white sandwich bread, crusts removed

1 cup milk

2lb good sausage meat (eg veal and pork)

1 free-range egg, beaten

1 tbsp chopped parsley

$\frac{1}{2}$ tsp ground nutmeg

sea salt

freshly ground black pepper

12 medium-thick slices bacon

paprika salmon

Chili-lime chicken wings

Thai flavors—garlic, lime juice, cilantro, and chili—give chicken wings a boost, turning them into an easy lunch. Serve with a sweet, sticky chili and lime dipping sauce.

Cut off the tips of the chicken wings, and bend each wing until you can cut cleanly between the joints.

Roughly chop the cilantro stems and pound with the garlic, chili pepper, salt, and sugar until you have a rough paste. Add the fish sauce or soy sauce, lime juice, and oil, and stir well. Rub this marinade all over the chicken pieces and marinate in the refrigerator for a couple of hours or overnight, turning once or twice.

Heat the oven to 425°F. Place the chicken on a foil-lined roasting pan and bake for 30 minutes until crisp and golden. Or grill on a ridged cast-iron griddle pan or over hot coals, turning once.

To make the chili-lime sauce, heat the sugar, vinegar, and sliced chili pepper in a saucepan, stirring until the sugar has dissolved. Bring to a boil and let bubble and reduce for a few minutes until the sauce is syrupy. Remove from the heat and add the lime juice, fish sauce, and cilantro leaves.

Drizzle the chicken wings with the chili-lime sauce and serve with lime quarters.

SERVES 4

8 medium chicken wings

4 cilantro stems

4 garlic cloves

1 small, hot red or green chili pepper

1 tsp salt

1 tsp sugar

2 tbsp Thai fish sauce or soy sauce

2 tbsp lime juice

2 tbsp vegetable oil

Chili-lime sauce:

½ cup sugar

½ cup white vinegar

1 small, hot red chili pepper, sliced

2 tbsp lime juice

2 tbsp Thai fish sauce

2 tbsp cilantro leaves

To serve:

lime quarters

Paprika salmon

This is a smart way of cooking salmon for a special lunch, spiking it with paprika oil and serving it simply, with roasted red bell peppers, capers, and watercress.

Heat the oven to 425°F. Lightly oil the peppers, then roast them for 20 minutes until scorched. Transfer the peppers to a bowl, cover, and set aside. Place a good, solid baking sheet in the oven to heat up for 3 minutes.

Mix the olive oil with the paprika, salt, and pepper. Coat the salmon with the spiced oil. Lightly oil the hot baking sheet and place the salmon on it, skin-side down. Bake for 10 to 12 minutes; the salmon should still be a little pink inside.

When the peppers are cool enough to handle, peel off the skin and cut the flesh into strips, discarding the core and seeds. Rinse the watercress, shake dry, and discard the thicker stems.

To make the dressing, whisk the ingredients together, with salt and pepper, until slightly thickened. Toss the watercress in the dressing and place on warmed dinner plates. Lay the seared salmon, skin-side up, on the cress, and arrange the peppers and capers on top.

SERVES 4
2 red bell peppers
2 tbsp extra virgin olive oil,
plus extra to oil peppers
1 tsp paprika
sea salt
freshly ground black pepper
6 thick pieces of salmon fillet,
around 7oz each
8oz watercress
1 tbsp small capers, rinsed

Dressing:
2 tbsp extra virgin olive oil
1 tbsp lemon juice or red
wine vinegar
1 tsp sugar

Fish in a bag

**When you cook fish in a sealed foil bag, it retains all its
delicacy and flavor. Add cherry tomatoes, spinach — or fine
green beans or asparagus — and garlic to the bag and you get
a complete meal with no mess and no fuss.**

Wash the spinach leaves well and shake dry. Heat the oven to
425°F. Cut out four 15-inch squares of foil.

Divide the spinach leaves among the foil squares. Season the fish
well with salt and pepper, and place on the spinach. Toss the
cherry tomatoes and garlic with the olive oil, salt, and pepper, and
spoon on top of the fish.

Bring two opposite sides of foil up to meet in the middle, and crimp
tightly from the middle to the outer edge, shaping into a half-moon
as you go. Now fold the crimped edge over again, squeezing it
tightly so air cannot escape. Bake for 15 minutes until the bag has
puffed up like a balloon.

Snip open each parcel, drain off most of the juices, and slide the
contents onto warm dinner plates. Drizzle with olive oil and serve
with lemon wedges.

SERVES 4
8 oz spinach leaves
(grown-up, not baby)
4 thick pieces of white fish
fillet (eg cod, haddock),
each 6 oz
sea salt
freshly ground pepper
8 oz cherry tomatoes
2 garlic cloves, thinly sliced
2 tbsp extra virgin olive oil,
plus extra to drizzle
1 lemon, quartered

Salt-grilled sardines

Long after the vacation bills have been paid and the suntan has faded, you can relive the memories of meals eaten by the sea or among the grape vines. These sardines take me right back to the smoky al fresco grills of the old Alfama district of Lisbon. And to think some people force themselves to eat oil-rich sardines and mackerel purely for their health.

Coat the bell peppers with some of the olive oil, and grill or broil, turning occasionally, until scorched and blistered all over. Peel off the skin and cut the peppers into long strips, discarding the core and seeds.

Brush the sardines and the grill rack with oil to help prevent sticking. Roll the sardines in the sea salt, pepper, and cayenne.

Grill over hot coals (or under the broiler) lightly on one side, then turn the sardines while they are still firm enough to be moved without breaking up. Grill on the other side until the skin is scorched and bubbling.

Arrange the grilled sardines and peppers on serving plates. Add a drizzle of extra virgin olive oil and serve with a wedge of lemon.

SERVES 4

2 red bell peppers

2 tbsp olive oil

8 large or 12 medium sardines, or small herring, gutted, cleaned, and scaled

1 tsp flaked sea salt (eg Maldon)

$\frac{1}{2}$ tsp freshly ground black pepper

pinch of cayenne pepper

a little extra virgin olive oil

1 lemon, quartered

bread

Cherry tomato bruschetta Toss 8oz cherry tomatoes in 1 tbsp olive oil and bake at 350°F for 20 minutes. Smash some garlic cloves in extra virgin olive oil, with sea salt and pepper. Toast 4 thick slices of sourdough bread under the broiler, brush with the oil, and top with the cherry tomatoes. Drizzle with more garlicky olive oil and serve.

Crostini with anchovies and capers Mash 8 canned anchovy fillets in oil with 1 tbsp rinsed capers, 1 tbsp minced parsley, and pepper. Mix to a paste by adding oil from the anchovy can, and spread on 2 big slices of toasted sourdough bread. Heat under the broiler, then cut into fingers.

Turn soup into zuppa Toast thick slices of sourdough bread, brush with garlicky olive oil, and place a slice in each bowl. Pour a simple vegetable and bean soup on top and serve. Try it scattered with grated cheese, too.

Cheat's pizza Spread 4 pita, naan, or Turkish flat breads with tomato salsa. Top with torn bocconcini (mozzarella balls), halved cherry tomatoes, anchovy fillets, and dried oregano. Drizzle with extra virgin olive oil and bake at 350°F for 8 minutes, or heat under the broiler.

Crumbs! Mix 3 tbsp fresh bread crumbs with 1 tbsp butter, 1 tsp lemon juice, $1/2$ tsp ground cumin, salt, and pepper. Spoon onto mussels, oysters, or sardines before broiling, or on fish or chicken fillets before baking.

Little marmalade toasts Beat 1 cup mascarpone with 1 tbsp sugar, 1 tbsp bitter orange marmalade, and 1 tbsp Cointreau or Scotch whisky. Finely slice a baguette and toast lightly on both sides under the broiler. Spread with a little marmalade, and top with the marmalade mascarpone. Serve with espresso coffee at a brunch party, or after dinner.

Peach bruschetta Cut a dry baguette into two 6-inch long sections, split in half lengthwise, and lightly butter. Crush 4 peeled, ripe peaches or 8 apricots onto the bread, scatter with raspberries, and sprinkle with 1 tbsp sugar. Bake at 350°F for 10 to 15 minutes until the bread is crisp. Dust with confectioners' sugar and serve as a dessert with crème fraîche.

Baked feta bread Slash a long baguette (as for garlic bread). Crush 2 garlic cloves in 2 tbsp olive oil with a few rosemary sprigs. Cut 7oz feta cheese into slices, coat in the oil, and wedge into each cut. Wrap in foil and bake at 350°F for 10 minutes until hot.

Prosciutto croissants Cut 4 large croissants horizontally in half, and lightly toast the cut sides. Cover with sliced prosciutto and top with sliced bocconcini (mozzarella). Broil briefly until the cheese is soft, and serve hot.

Italian bread salad Toast 2 thick slices of country-style bread and cut into cubes. Combine with 1 minced red bell pepper, 1 tbsp rinsed capers, 1 crushed garlic clove, 2 anchovy fillets, 1 tbsp black olives, 2 tbsp red wine vinegar, and 3 tbsp extra virgin olive oil, and toss.

Avocado and lime toast Crush the flesh of 1 ripe avocado with a pinch of sea salt and a big squeeze of lime juice. Toast 2 thick slices of sourdough bread and brush with garlicky olive oil. Spread the avocado thickly on top and add plenty of black pepper. A brilliant breakfast for two.

Chocolate French toast Make a batter by beating 2 eggs with 2 tbsp sugar, $^1/_2$ cup milk, and 1 tsp cinnamon. Dip 4 thick slices of stale ciabatta (Italian slipper bread) in the batter and fry in 1 tbsp butter until golden and crisp. Drizzle with hot chocolate sauce or dip into mugs of hot chocolate.

peach bruschetta

dinner

Chinese roast pork

This isn't as scary as you might think. Fresh side pork, or belly, which is really uncured slab bacon, is usually available from Asian markets. It is the easiest roast in the world, giving you tender meat topped with lots of crisp cracklings. Serve sliced with steamed rice and Chinese greens, or cut into fingers to dip into hoisin sauce as an appetizer.

Wash and dry the pork, then score the skin at $1/2$-inch intervals (for easy slicing later). Combine the salt and five spice powder, and rub all over the skin and meat. Set aside in the refrigerator for at least 2 hours.

SERVES 4

$2^1/4$-lb piece fresh side pork

1 tbsp salt

1 tbsp Chinese five spice powder

$1/4$ cup hoisin sauce

Heat the oven to 450°F. Line a roasting pan with foil and place the pork on a rack set above the foil. Roast for 20 minutes.

Lower the oven setting to 400°F and roast for 45 more minutes or until the skin crackles and crisps. If it doesn't totally crisp, finish under the broiler, being careful not to let the skin blister too much.

Remove the pork from the oven, and cut out any bones from the base. Cut the pork into thick slices, and then into thick fingers if you like. Serve warm, with hoisin sauce for dipping.

Pork chop with capers

A caper is a frisky leap or a dance. It's also the unopened flower bud of *Capparis spinosa*, a straggly, unkempt Mediterranean shrub. When cured, each little bud has the same sort of frisky effect in the mouth, especially in this lemony parsley dressing. Serve with an arugula salad and potatoes or a squash mash.

To cook the pork chops, heat the olive oil in a nonstick frying pan. Lightly dust the chops in the flour, seasoned with salt, pepper, and paprika or cayenne; shake off any excess. Cook on one side over a moderate heat for around 8 minutes. Turn and cook on the other side for 5 minutes or until tender.

To make the dressing, pick the leaves from the parsley stems. Halve the tomato, squeeze out the seeds and juice, and finely chop the flesh. Mix the chopped tomato with the capers, parsley leaves, olive oil, and lemon juice. Season with sea salt and pepper, and stir well.

Season the pork chops and place on warmed serving plates. Use a slotted spoon to spoon the dressing on and around each pork chop. Top with caper berries.

SERVES 4
4 large pork rib chops
2 tbsp olive oil
2 tbsp all-purpose flour
$\frac{1}{2}$ tsp sea salt
$\frac{1}{2}$ tsp freshly ground black pepper
$\frac{1}{2}$ tsp smoked paprika or cayenne pepper
8 caper berries

Dressing:
large handful of flat-leaf parsley
1 ripe, red tomato
1 tbsp capers, rinsed
3 tbsp extra virgin olive oil
1 tbsp lemon juice

Ham and mushroom pie

A nice big pie all to myself is my idea of comfort food, especially when frozen puff pastry makes it so simple.

Heat the oven to 400°F. Strip the thyme leaves from their stems. Heat the olive oil in a frying pan and gently cook the onion, garlic, and thyme for 5 minutes. Slice the mushrooms, add to the pan, and cook for 10 minutes until soft.

Shred the cooked ham or chicken, discarding any bones or skin. Off the heat, add to the mushroom mixture with the cooked peas. Season well with salt and pepper.

To make the sauce, melt the butter in a small saucepan, add the flour, and cook, stirring, over a gentle heat for 3 minutes. Add a few spoonfuls of chicken stock and stir well, then add the remaining stock and bring to a boil, stirring constantly as the sauce thickens.

Add the cream, Worcestershire sauce, mustard, nutmeg, and cayenne. Simmer gently for a couple of minutes, stirring. Add salt and pepper to taste, then strain the sauce over the filling and toss well to mix.

Divide the filling among four individual baking dishes. Cover the tops with pastry, trimming to fit. Brush with beaten egg and bake for 30 minutes until puffy and golden.

MAKES 4

6 thyme sprigs
1 tbsp olive oil
1 onion, minced
2 garlic cloves, smashed
1 lb button mushrooms
1 lb cooked ham or chicken
1⅓ cups shelled fresh or frozen green peas, cooked
sea salt
freshly ground black pepper
1 lb ready-rolled frozen puff pastry, thawed
1 free-range egg, beaten

Sauce:
1 tbsp butter
1 tbsp all-purpose flour
1 cup chicken stock
2 tbsp cream
1 tbsp Worcestershire sauce
1 tsp Dijon mustard
½ tsp ground nutmeg
½ tsp cayenne pepper

drunken potatoes

Lamb with tomatoes and olives

I grew up with the time-honored roast lamb every Sunday, followed by variations on a theme of lamb most evenings during the week. You'd think I'd be over it, but instead I love cooking lamb at home, and ordering lamb when eating out. This is typical of the sort of thing I do at home when I'm pushed for time.

Place the lamb steaks between two sheets of plastic wrap or wax paper and bash them flatter with a meat pounder or rolling pin. Place in a shallow dish and toss with the olive oil, garlic, and rosemary sprigs.

SERVES 4

4 boneless lamb leg steaks,
   around 6oz each
2 tbsp extra virgin olive oil
2 garlic cloves, smashed
2 rosemary sprigs
sea salt
freshly ground black pepper
8oz cherry tomatoes
$^2/_3$ cup small black olives
   (eg Niçoise or Ligurian)

Heat a nonstick frying pan. When it is very hot, add the lamb (saving the marinade) and sear very quickly for a minute or two on each side, turning once. Remove the lamb to a plate while still pink inside, season with salt and pepper, and let rest for a minute or two while you do the tomatoes.

Tip the reserved marinade into the pan, and add the cherry tomatoes and olives. Warm through until the tomatoes start to soften and burst.

Slice the lamb and arrange on warm plates. Tip the tomatoes and olives over the lamb and serve.

Drunken potatoes

This is my favorite new way of roasting potatoes, because they absorb the flavor of the white wine they're cooked in, then turn crisp at the edges. For all those who loved the crash hot potatoes that appeared in *Simple Food*, you owe it to yourself to move on. Serve these with grilled or pan-fried meat, poultry, or fish, such as lamb with tomatoes (left), salt and pepper steak (page 80), jump-in-the-pan chicken (page 85), or cod in prosciutto (page 90).

Heat the oven to 400°F. Peel the potatoes and finely slice crosswise. Toss the potato slices in a bowl with the olive oil, salt, and pepper. Lightly oil a shallow roasting pan and scatter the potatoes loosely over the bottom. Pour the white wine over and scatter with the thyme.

Bake for 30 minutes, during which time the wine will boil and bubble away, and the potatoes will crisp to a beautiful golden crunch. Keep an eye on them during the last few minutes after the wine has evaporated, as they can over-crisp. The slices in the corners might get scorched, but it's worth the sacrifice.

Use a slotted spatula to lift the potatoes out of the pan. Serve hot.

SERVES 4

3 large, long potatoes, around 1$^1/_2$lb

2 tbsp extra virgin olive oil

sea salt

freshly ground black pepper

1 cup dry white wine

1 tbsp thyme sprigs

Salt and pepper steak

One of the tricks of good, simple cooking is to upgrade your salt and pepper. I love soft-flaked Maldon sea salt, and buy fresh-tasting vine-ripened peppercorns from India. Sea salt is added to this pepper-crusted steak after cooking, not before, as it would draw out the juices from the meat. Serve with wilted spinach and potatoes.

Crush the peppercorns, then place in a fine sieve and shake to discard any fine dust. Tip the pepper onto a flat plate and press one side of each steak only into the mixture.

Heat the olive oil in a heavy, nonstick frying pan. When hot, add the steaks, pepper-side down, and cook for 3 minutes over moderate heat, without moving them. Turn and cook for 2 to 3 more minutes, depending on thickness. Transfer the steaks to warm plates.

SERVES 2

1 tbsp black peppercorns

2 boneless sirloin steaks, 7oz each

1 tbsp olive oil

2 tbsp butter

1 tbsp brandy or Cognac

$\frac{1}{3}$ cup heavy cream

2 tsp Dijon mustard

sea salt (eg Maldon)

Add the butter to the pan and melt. Add the brandy (carefully, as it might flame), stirring well. Add the cream, mustard, and a pinch of salt, stirring briskly as it bubbles. Pour into a warm pitcher. Scatter extra sea salt on the steaks and serve with the mustard sauce.

Korean beef in lettuce

Tender beef is marinated in soy, garlic, ginger, green onions, and sesame oil, then flash-fried—so quickly that you need everyone waiting at the table before you begin.

Slice the beef thinly, against the grain. For the marinade, finely slice the green onions and mix with the other ingredients; stir to dissolve the sugar. Add the beef, turn to coat, and marinate for 1 hour or so.

Wash and dry the lettuce leaves; chill. For the soy-chili sauce, mix the sauces together in a bowl and set aside. Cook the jasmine rice until tender; keep warm.

Heat a heavy frying pan. When hot, sear the beef over high heat for 1 to 2 minutes, leaving it still pink in the middle. Scatter with the sesame seeds and serve on warm plates, with the rice and lettuce.

Spoon a little jasmine rice onto a lettuce leaf, add a slice or two of spicy beef and a little soy-chili sauce, wrap the lettuce leaf around the filling, and eat in the hands.

SERVES 4
2 boneless sirloin steaks,
1-inch thick and
around 8oz each
8 butter lettuce leaves
1 cup jasmine rice
1 tbsp sesame seeds

Marinade:
2 green onions
2 garlic cloves, crushed
2-inch piece of fresh
ginger, grated
1 tbsp toasted sesame oil
2 tbsp rice wine or dry sherry
3 tbsp soy sauce
1 tbsp Chinese sweet chili
sauce or chili bean paste
1/2 tsp ground black pepper
1 tbsp sugar

Soy-chili sauce:
2 tbsp soy sauce
2 tbsp Chinese sweet chili
sauce or chili bean paste

Jump-in-the-pan chicken

This is an action dish, a simple sauté in the pan that creates its own creamy lemon and caper sauce for chicken. It's a terrific idea when you bring home the usual chicken breast and want to do something really fast. The trick is to keep the pan moving, jiggling it on the heat to make the chicken jump. Serve with rice, noodles, or mashed potato, or a green salad.

Place each chicken breast between two sheets of plastic wrap or wax paper and bash flat with a meat pounder or rolling pin, and I mean as thin as a coin—almost breaking up.

Tear the chicken into little rags with your fingers, and toss lightly in the flour, seasoned with salt and pepper.

Heat the olive oil and butter in a large, heavy-based frying pan. When hot, add the chicken, scattering the pieces so they don't clump together. Instead of stirring, move the pan on the heat and flip the chicken pieces until lightly golden, so they jump in the pan.

Add the garlic, bay leaves, capers, sea salt, and pepper. Remove the pan from the heat, add the wine, and return to a high heat. Let the wine bubble away, again jiggling the pan like crazy.

When there is only a little wine left, add the lemon juice and parsley leaves, and jiggle the pan until the sauce comes together and looks creamy. Serve immediately.

SERVES 4

3 skinless chicken breast halves, around 5oz each

2 tbsp all-purpose flour

sea salt

freshly ground black pepper

2 tbsp olive oil

1 tbsp butter

1 garlic clove, crushed

4 bay leaves

2 tbsp capers, well rinsed

½ cup dry white wine

1 tbsp lemon juice

2 tbsp flat-leaf parsley leaves

Chicken and chickpea stew

A very satisfying chicken stew, this takes some of the typical ingredients and flavors of Spain — sherry, paprika, chorizo sausages — and turns them into a lively, spicy winter meal you can have on the table within an hour of walking in the door.

Peel the carrots and potatoes, and cut into bite-sized pieces. Dust the chicken lightly with flour, seasoned with salt and pepper. Heat 2 tbsp olive oil in a heavy frying pan and brown the chicken pieces.

Add the garlic, carrots, potatoes, paprika, bay leaves, salt, and pepper. Add the sherry and water and bring to a boil, then simmer, covered, for about 20 minutes. Add the chickpeas, and cook for 10 more minutes or until the chicken is tender.

Thickly slice the chorizo and pan-fry in the remaining oil until sizzling. Add to the stew, scatter with parsley, and serve.

SERVES 4

3 medium carrots

1 lb potatoes

8 chicken pieces (eg legs, thighs, breast halves)

1 tbsp all-purpose flour

sea salt

freshly ground black pepper

3 tbsp olive oil

2 garlic cloves, smashed

1 tsp paprika

2 bay leaves

½ cup dry sherry

1 cup water

14 oz canned chickpeas (garbanzo beans), drained and rinsed

2 chorizo sausages, mild or hot

2 tbsp flat-leaf parsley leaves

cod in prosciutto

Cod in prosciutto

Any firm, white-fleshed fish can be cooked in this way. The outer covering of prosciutto or bacon protects the fish and gives a good crisp texture. Simple, really. Serve with shredded cabbage and plenty of mashed potato.

Trim the cod fillets into neat squares, season well, and wrap in the prosciutto or bacon. Heat the oil in a frying pan and cook the fish on both sides until the prosciutto is lightly browned and the fish is cooked through, about 4 minutes each side, depending on thickness.

Discard the outer cabbage leaves, cut out any core, and finely shred the rest. Cook in simmering salted water for 5 minutes—the cabbage should have a soft crunch but still retain a bright color. Drain well, return to the dry pan, and toss with the butter or olive oil, vinegar, sugar, fennel or caraway seeds, sea salt, and pepper.

Spoon the cabbage onto four warmed dinner plates, place the pan-fried fish on top, and scatter with the thyme or parsley.

SERVES 4

4 pieces of cod fillet, around
    6 oz each

sea salt

freshly ground black pepper

4 wide or 8 thin slices
    prosciutto or bacon

1 tbsp olive oil

1/2 head Savoy cabbage,
    around 1 lb

2 tbsp butter or olive oil

1 tbsp red wine vinegar

1 tsp sugar

1 tsp fennel or caraway seeds

few thyme sprigs or parsley
    leaves

Insalata di mare

I love the Italian way with a seafood salad—all relaxed, sunny, and easy—using good-flavored olive oil and simple herbs. Chickpeas aren't usually served with seafood, but I can't for the life of me think why not.

Scrub the mussels or clams, discarding any that don't close when sharply tapped. Rinse the squid well and cut the tubes into 1½-inch pieces. Score the insides lightly to help them curl.

Heat the olive oil, wine, peppercorns, garlic, and parsley stems in a heavy pan. Add the mussels, cover tightly, and turn up the heat. Shake the pan after a minute or two, and take out any mussels that have opened. Repeat twice, then discard any that haven't opened.

Strain the broth and return to the pan. Add the chickpeas and cook for 5 minutes. Add the squid and simmer for 1 minute or until just tender. Remove the squid and chickpeas with a slotted spoon and gently toss with the mussels, lemon juice, extra virgin olive oil, pepper, and parsley. Add a spoonful or two of the seafood broth and serve warm or at room temperature, with lemon wedges.

SERVES 4
2¼ lb fresh mussels or clams
1 lb cleaned small squid
(calamari)
2 tbsp olive oil
1 cup white wine
6 black peppercorns
2 garlic cloves, smashed
4 parsley stems
14 oz canned chickpeas
(garbanzo beans),
drained and rinsed
2 tbsp lemon juice
2 tbsp extra virgin olive oil
freshly ground black pepper
1 tbsp flat-leaf parsley leaves
1 lemon, quartered

Goat cheese cannelloni

Rolling sheets of lasagne around a creamy cheese filling is a lot easier than stuffing cannelloni pasta tubes.

Heat the oven to 350°F. Bring a pot of salted water to a boil. Add the lasagne sheets, one at a time, and cook at a rolling boil until pliable, around 6 minutes. Drain and lay on a dry dish towel.

To make the filling, mash the ricotta, goat cheese, parsley, chives, salt, pepper, and nutmeg together in a bowl.

Lay one sheet of lasagne on a board, spoon some of the mixture across the middle, and roll into a cylinder. Place in a lightly greased baking dish. Repeat with the remaining lasagne and filling, laying the filled cannelloni side by side in the dish.

To make the sauce, whiz the tomatoes and their juice with the olive oil, sugar, salt, and pepper in a blender. Add the chopped herbs.

Pour the sauce over the cannelloni to cover completely. Scatter with parmesan and thyme, and bake for 30 minutes until bubbling hot.

SERVES 4
8 dried lasagne sheets
1 1/2 cups fresh ricotta cheese
4 oz soft, fresh goat cheese
2 tbsp minced parsley
2 tsp minced chives
1/2 tsp salt
1/2 tsp freshly ground black pepper
1/2 tsp ground nutmeg
2 tbsp finely grated parmesan
10 thyme sprigs

Sauce:
14 oz canned crushed tomatoes
1 tbsp olive oil
1 tsp sugar
1 tbsp chopped parsley
1 tbsp chopped thyme leaves

vegetables

Cabbage with cumin

How to turn a cabbage-hater into a cabbage-lover: buy the smallest, brightest, crispest, and heaviest cabbage you can find, preferably the crinkly-leafed Savoy, cook it quickly, and serve in a vinaigrette with cumin seeds.

Bring a large pan of water to a boil. Trim the base of the cabbage, but don't cut out the entire core as this will hold the wedges together. Cut the cabbage in half from top to bottom and then cut each half into three equal wedges. Discard the outer leaves that aren't up to scratch.

Add the salt to the boiling water and cook the cabbage wedges for 5 to 10 minutes or until they start to soften. Drain them well, upside down in a colander.

SERVES 4 TO 6

1 small, tight head Savoy
   cabbage, around 2 lb

1/2 tsp salt

1 tbsp olive oil

1 tbsp white wine vinegar

1 tsp sugar

sea salt

freshly ground black pepper

2 tsp cumin or caraway seeds

Whisk the olive oil, wine vinegar, sugar, sea salt, and pepper together in a bowl to make a vinaigrette. Arrange the cabbage on a serving platter and spoon the vinaigrette over. Scatter with the cumin or caraway seeds and serve.

Pumpkin with raclette

Naturally sweet vegetables, such as pumpkin and butternut squash, are fantastic teamed with cheese. Raclette, fontina, and taleggio are all good melting cheeses, or use fresh mozzarella. Serve with a simple roast or a leafy green vegetable.

Heat the oven to 400°F. Cut the pumpkin or squash roughly into 1-inch cubes, cutting off any skin and discarding the seeds.

Steam the pumpkin or squash cubes over fast boiling water for 20 minutes until tender, then drain and pile into a heatproof bowl or gratin dish. (If you don't have a steamer, put the cubes in a roasting pan, add a dash of water, cover with foil, and bake for 30 minutes or until tender.)

Cut the cheese into thin slices. Bake the pumpkin for 10 minutes or so, to help dry out the rather watery flesh (this isn't necessary with butternut squash), then top with the slices of cheese and bake for another minute or two until melted. Scatter with sea salt, pepper, oregano, sage, and thyme, and serve.

SERVES 4
2¼-lb piece of pumpkin or
butternut squash
5oz raclette or other
melting cheese
sea salt
freshly ground black pepper
few oregano sprigs
1 tbsp sage leaves
few thyme sprigs

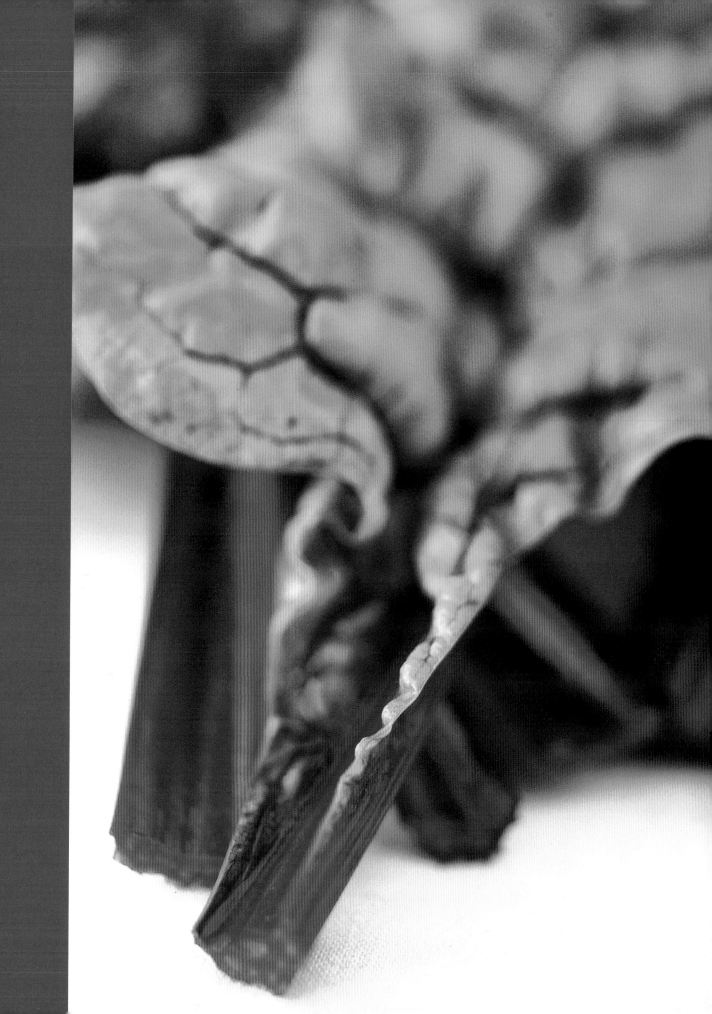

beets and greens

Green vegetable frittata

A frittata is an Italian-style flat omelette that makes a simple lunch or supper. Use Swiss chard, ruby or rainbow chard, cavolo nero (Italian black cabbage), or even green vegetables such as leeks, asparagus, green peas, and fine green beans.

Cut the stems from the chard and roughly chop. Cook in a large pot of simmering salted water for 10 minutes. Wash the leaves well, roughly chop, and add to the pot. Cook for 3 or 4 minutes until wilted. Drain well and cool, then squeeze out any excess water.

Beat the eggs, yolks, cream, cheese, salt, pepper, and nutmeg in a bowl. Heat the butter and oil in a nonstick frying pan (with heatproof handle), then pour in the eggs. Scatter in the greens, jiggling them so they settle in evenly. Cook over moderate heat until the frittata has set on the base and is lightly golden. Heat the broiler.

Broil the frittata for a few minutes until lightly golden and just set in the middle. If it's still runny, cover the pan and place over a moderate heat for a minute or two. Cut into big wedges and serve.

SERVES 4 TO 6

2 lb Swiss chard

6 free-range eggs, plus
   2 extra egg yolks

$^{1}/_{2}$ cup light cream

$^{3}/_{4}$ cup freshly grated
   parmesan or gruyère

sea salt

freshly ground black pepper

$^{1}/_{2}$ tsp freshly grated nutmeg

1 tsp butter

2 tsp olive oil

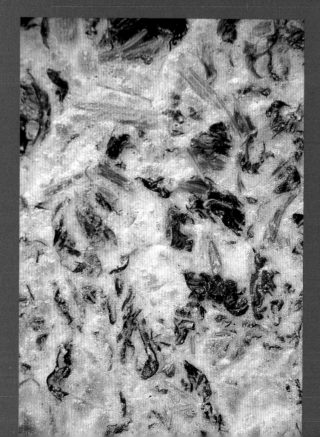

Beets and greens

Buying baby beets without their ruby red stems and small, bright green leaves is like buying asparagus without the tips. If the tops have already been guillotined, serve the beets on wilted spinach leaves or Swiss chard.

Cut the baby beets from their stems and cook, unpeeled, in simmering salted water for around 45 minutes until tender. Drain and cool, then rub off the skin with your fingers. Rinse well. Toss the beets in 1 tbsp of the extra virgin olive oil and set aside.

Wash the leafy stems, and discard the thickest parts of the stems. Roughly chop the leaves and stems, keeping them separate.

Cook the stems in boiling salted water for 2 minutes, then add the leaves and cover. Simmer for 3 minutes until the leaves have wilted and the stems are tender. Drain well, and toss with the remaining extra virgin olive oil, the lemon juice, sea salt, and pepper.

Arrange on a large platter and tumble the baby beets on top. Serve warm or at room temperature with lemon wedges, as a side dish. Or, serve as part of a meal of shared plates, perhaps with marinated feta, grilled lamb, and a tomato and cucumber salad.

SERVES 4
12 baby beets, with leaves
$1/2$ tsp salt
3 tbsp extra virgin olive oil
1 tbsp lemon juice
sea salt
freshly ground black pepper
1 lemon, quartered

Caponata

This is essentially a sweet and sour vegetable stew that began in the "caupona," a type of osteria or tavern in southern Italy, which serves cooked vegetables. Local sailors bought the vegetables while in port, then ate them flavored with vinegar and sugar when at sea. Serve with lightly warmed pita bread or flat bread.

Cut the eggplants into thick slices, then cut each slice into roughly $1/2$-inch cubes. Heat 2 tbsp olive oil in a frying pan and fry the eggplant briskly, tossing well, until golden and half cooked. Remove with a slotted spoon and set aside.

Add the rest of the olive oil to the frying pan. When hot, add the onion and cook for 5 minutes until soft.

In the meantime, cut the tomatoes in half and squeeze out the seeds. Roughly chop the tomato flesh and add to the pan with the eggplant, celery, bay leaf, olives, salt, and pepper. Cook for 10 more minutes.

Dissolve the sugar in the wine vinegar and add to the pan along with the capers. Cook for 10 more minutes until the eggplant is soft and there is no longer a sharp taste of vinegar.

Lightly toast the pine nuts in a hot, dry pan. Lightly warm the bread in a moderate oven or in a hot, dry pan for 2 minutes. Scatter the pine nuts over the vegetables, drizzle with olive oil, and serve at room temperature, with a pile of warm bread.

SERVES 4 TO 6
2 medium eggplants
3 tbsp olive oil
1 onion, minced
4 medium tomatoes
2 celery stalks, finely sliced
1 bay leaf
3 tbsp green olives, pitted
sea salt
freshly ground black pepper
1 tbsp sugar
2 tbsp red wine vinegar
1 tbsp capers, rinsed
2 tbsp pine nuts

To serve:
6-8 flat or pita breads
extra virgin olive oil

Mallorcan tumbet

I came across these layered baked vegetables in Mallorca, where they are cooked in a terracotta "cassola." I'm all for using canned tomatoes to make a sauce, especially in winter.

To make the sauce, combine the tomatoes, oregano, garlic, and olive oil with sea salt and pepper in a saucepan, and simmer, covered, for 20 minutes. Heat the oven to 350°F.

Peel and finely slice the potatoes. Finely slice the eggplants. Cut the peppers into long thin fingers, discarding core and seeds. Heat 2 tbsp olive oil in a frying pan and gently fry the potatoes, in batches, until golden on both sides. Layer in a 1-quart baking dish and season.

Add the remaining oil to the pan and fry the eggplant until well browned. Arrange over the potatoes and season. Fry the red peppers, then layer on top of the eggplant.

Spoon the tomato sauce over the top of the vegetables and bake for 20 minutes until bubbling hot. Serve warm or at room temperature, as an appetizer or side dish, or as a main course for two.

SERVES 4

1 lb all-purpose potatoes

1 lb eggplants

2 red bell peppers

3 tbsp olive oil

sea salt

freshly ground black pepper

Sauce:

14 oz canned crushed tomatoes

3 oregano sprigs, or 1 tsp dried oregano

3 garlic cloves, finely sliced

2 tbsp olive oil

Peas and bacon

Peas should be revered as they were in the seventeenth century, when the sophisticated Madame de Maintenon from the French court of Louis XIV wrote of the royal courtiers' obsession with peas as "both a fashion and a madness."

Cook the peas in simmering salted water until just tender. Drain, refresh with cold water, drain well again, and set aside. (You can do this ahead of time.)

SERVES 4

4 cups shelled fresh or frozen green peas

salt

6 shallots, or 1 small red onion

4 thick bacon slices, around 4 oz

2 tbsp butter

½ cup chicken stock or dry white wine

1 tsp sugar

sea salt

freshly ground black pepper

Peel and slice the shallots or onion, and mince the bacon. Heat half the butter in a pan and gently cook the shallots and bacon for 5 minutes. Add the stock or wine and bring to a boil, then reduce to a simmer.

Add the peas, sugar, sea salt, plenty of black pepper, and the remaining butter. Gently simmer until the liquid is reduced to a couple of tablespoonfuls, then serve.

Paper-bag vegetables

Paper-bag vegetables

A splendid vegetarian dinner is in the bag with these baked paper "purses" of steamy spiced vegetables, served with a bowl of garlicky herbed crème fraîche. You need parchment paper to make the bags.

Heat the oven to 400°F. Trim the leeks and cut into ½-inch slices. Peel the potatoes, sweet potato, and parsnips, and cut into chunky bite-sized pieces. Cut the zucchini and red pepper into similar pieces, discarding the pepper core and seeds.

In a large bowl, mix the olive oil with the saffron, thyme, rosemary, salt, and pepper. Add the vegetables and toss well.

SERVES 4

2 leeks

4 smallish potatoes

1 medium sweet potato

2 medium parsnips

2 medium zucchini

1 red bell pepper

4 tbsp extra virgin olive oil

½ tsp powdered saffron

4 thyme sprigs

4 rosemary sprigs

sea salt

freshly ground black pepper

1 tbsp fennel seeds

To serve:

2 garlic cloves, crushed

2 tbsp minced parsley

1 cup crème fraîche

Cut four rounds of parchment paper, each 14 inches in diameter. Divide the vegetables among them and scatter with fennel seeds. Bring the paper up evenly around each pile of vegetables, pursing it together at the top and tying securely with string.

Place the bags on a baking sheet and bake for 30 to 40 minutes or until an inserted skewer meets with no resistance. Meanwhile, beat the garlic and parsley into the crème fraîche and set aside.

To serve, snip the paper parcels open below the string, and serve in or out of the paper, with the herbed crème fraîche.

Black-olive roasted vegetables

I always keep a jar of pesto and a jar of olive tapenade in the refrigerator door next to the Campari and soda. They're great instant flavor hits if you don't want to do much more than toast some sourdough bread or cook some pasta for dinner.

Heat the oven to 400°F. Cut the pumpkin into thinnish wedges, trim off the skin, and discard any seeds. Peel the potatoes and cut in half. Wash the carrots, trim the tops neatly, and peel. Peel the parsnips and cut lengthwise into quarters.

Combine the tapenade with the olive oil and pepper in a big bowl. Add the vegetables, rosemary, and garlic cloves, and toss until well coated. Tip into a shallow roasting pan and bake for 45 minutes to 1 hour until the vegetables are tender and nicely browned.

Pile the roasted vegetables onto warm plates and tuck in a few fresh rosemary sprigs. Top with a spoonful of olive tapenade, thinned with a little olive oil.

SERVES 4
1-lb piece of pumpkin
1 lb smallish potatoes
2 bunches baby carrots
4 parsnips
2 tbsp black olive tapenade
2 tbsp extra virgin olive oil
1/2 tsp freshly ground black pepper
4 rosemary sprigs
4 garlic cloves (unpeeled)

To serve:
rosemary sprigs
extra black olive tapenade
a little extra virgin olive oil

Vegetable curry

For me, an Indian vegetable curry should be warmly spiced, rather than chili-hot, with meltingly soft vegetables, and a sauce that calls for a huge mound of rice. Used as a herb in cooking, curry leaves have a spicy flavor like curry powder.

Peel and roughly chop the potatoes. Peel and quarter the carrot and parsnips lengthwise. Cut the eggplant, zucchini, and red pepper into chunks, discarding the pepper core and seeds.

Heat the oil in a heavy-based frying pan and add the mustard and fenugreek seeds. When the seeds start to pop, add the cumin, turmeric, ginger, and paprika, stirring. Add the onion and cook for 5 minutes until softened.

Add the potatoes and fry lightly, then add the carrot, parsnips, eggplant, zucchini, and red pepper, stirring. Add the water or stock, tomato paste, salt, sugar, curry leaves, and cinnamon stick, and stir to mix. Bring to a boil.

Simmer, uncovered, for 30 to 40 minutes or until the vegetables are soft and the liquid is reduced to a sauce, stirring occasionally. Serve with plenty of rice.

SERVES 4

1 lb all-purpose potatoes

1 carrot, peeled

2 parsnips, peeled

1 eggplant

1 zucchini

1 red bell pepper

2 tbsp vegetable oil

2 tsp mustard seeds

$\frac{1}{2}$ tsp fenugreek seeds

1 tsp ground cumin

1 tsp ground turmeric

1 tsp ground ginger

$\frac{1}{2}$ tsp paprika

1 onion, finely sliced

4 cups water or stock

1 tbsp tomato paste

1 tsp salt

1 tsp brown sugar

few curry leaves (optional)

1 cinnamon stick

Potato and bean mash Cook 2lb potatoes with 2 peeled garlic cloves until tender, adding 14oz drained, canned cannellini beans for the last minute. Drain and return to the pan. Add 2 tbsp extra virgin olive oil, 1 tbsp chopped parsley, sea salt, and pepper. Mash, keeping it chunky.

Greek red potatoes Parboil 2lb peeled, quartered waxy potatoes for 10 minutes; drain. Toss with 2 tbsp tomato paste, 2 tbsp extra virgin olive oil, 2 tbsp water, salt, and pepper. Bake in a foil-lined pan at 400°F for 20 minutes until tender. Serve with roast lamb or broiled fish.

Mealy or waxy? Use dry, mealy potatoes such as russets or long whites for mashing, baking, and frying. Choose moist, waxy potatoes— round reds and round whites—and new potatoes for simple boiled potatoes and salads.

Warm saffron potato salad Whisk 2 tbsp extra virgin olive oil with 1 tbsp mayonnaise, 1 tbsp lemon juice, 1 tsp tomato paste, 1 tsp Dijon mustard, $^1/_2$ tsp powdered saffron, $^1/_2$ tsp paprika, sea salt, and pepper. Thickly slice 2lb boiled potatoes and toss in the dressing while still warm.

Potato, tuna, and olive salad Drain and flake 14oz canned tuna in oil. Whisk 3 tbsp extra virgin olive oil, 3 tbsp white wine, and 2 tbsp lemon juice with salt and pepper. Thickly slice 1$^1/_4$lb boiled potatoes and toss in the dressing. Add the tuna and 20 black olives. Serve with arugula.

Is it cooked? When you boil potatoes, spear one with a thin bamboo skewer so the stick pokes up out of the water. To check if the potatoes are cooked, pick up the bamboo stick. If the potato clings to it, it's not yet cooked. If it slips off, it's perfect. Brilliant!

Goose fat potatoes Peel 3 medium waxy potatoes and cut into $^3/_4$-inch dice. Fry gently in $^1/_2$ cup goose or duck fat with 2 peeled garlic cloves for 20 minutes, tossing occasionally, then turn up the heat and cook until crisp and brown. Drain, toss with sea salt and pepper, and serve.

Belgian stoemp Cook $1^1/_2$lb potatoes with 3 finely sliced leeks until tender. Drain and lightly mash with butter, salt, pepper, and a little grated nutmeg. Serve with sausages, broiled fish, or a thick slice of baked ham.

Herring and potato salad Dress $1^1/_4$lb hot boiled potatoes with 2 tbsp olive oil, 2 tbsp white wine, 2 tbsp red wine vinegar, and 1 tbsp Dijon mustard. Add a dollop of sour cream, 1 tbsp capers, lots of pepper, and a little finely sliced shallot. Drape 4 marinated herrings on top.

Choucroute for cheats Cook 2lb small peeled potatoes until tender. Heat $1^1/_4$ cups prepared sauerkraut in a pan with 1 tsp caraway seeds and $^1/_2$ cup white wine. Simmer 4 frankfurters and 4 weisswurst (or 8 frankfurters) for 5 minutes; drain and serve on the sauerkraut and potatoes, with German mustard.

Smoked salmon potato Prick 4 large baking potatoes, coat lightly in olive oil, and roll in a little sea salt and cracked black pepper. Bake at 400°F for $1^1/_2$ hours until soft. Cut open and top with crème fraîche, smoked salmon, horseradish sauce, and chives.

Six more baked potato toppings Bake 4 large potatoes (as above), and top with: poached egg and crisp bacon; caramelized onions; pan-fried mushrooms with chives; pan-fried chicken livers; wilted arugula with gorgonzola; or roasted red bell peppers tossed with capers and anchovies.

goose fat potatoes

family

Spicy pork noodles

This is the Chinese equivalent of spaghetti Bolognese. Unusual ingredients are available from Asian markets.

Mix the brown bean sauce, hoisin sauce, soy sauce, water, and sugar together in a bowl, stirring. Set aside.

Peel the cucumber, and pare lengthwise with a vegetable peeler into ribbons. Cut the ribbons into matchsticks and set aside.

SERVES 4

1 tbsp brown bean sauce or chili bean paste

1 tbsp hoisin sauce

2 tbsp soy sauce

$\frac{1}{2}$ cup water

1 tsp brown sugar

$\frac{1}{2}$ hothouse cucumber

2 tbsp peanut oil

4 green onions, minced

1 lb ground pork

1 tbsp cornstarch

1 tbsp water or Chinese rice wine

1 lb fresh oiled egg noodles (Hokkien)

Heat a wok or frying pan. When hot, add the oil and stir-fry most of the green onions for 30 seconds. Add the pork and stir-fry for a few minutes until browned. Add the sauce mix and stir-fry for about 5 minutes until the water has evaporated, oil rises to the surface, and the pork smells sweet and spicy. Mix the cornstarch with the water or rice wine and add to the meat, stirring.

Place the noodles in a large heatproof bowl and cover with boiling water. Drain well and return to the bowl. Add the spicy pork sauce and toss well. Divide among four deep, warmed bowls, scatter with cucumber and reserved green onions, and serve, with chopsticks.

Long life noodles

Cantonese legend has it that the longer the noodle, the longer you will live. Or it could just be that noodles are good for you.

Put the dried mushrooms in a bowl, pour on the boiling water, and let soak for at least 30 minutes. Cut the white leek into 2-inch lengths, halve lengthwise, and cut into very thin matchstick strips.

Lift the mushrooms from the water, discard the stems, and slice the caps finely; set aside. Strain ½ cup of the soaking water into a bowl and stir in the soy sauce, oyster sauce, sesame oil, and sugar; set aside. Place the noodles in a large heatproof bowl and pour boiling water over to cover. Drain well and set aside.

Heat a wok. When hot, add the oil and stir-fry the ginger and garlic for 1 minute. Add the leek and mushrooms, tossing well over high heat. Add the sauce, bring to a boil, and cook, stirring, for 1 minute.

Add the tofu and cook for 1 minute. Add the noodles and cook for about 2 minutes, tossing, until they have absorbed most of the sauce. Scatter with green onions and serve, with chopsticks.

SERVES 4

6 dried Chinese mushrooms
1 cup boiling water
1 leek, white part only
2 tbsp soy sauce
1 tbsp oyster sauce
1 tsp toasted sesame oil
1 tsp sugar
1 lb fresh oiled egg noodles (Hokkien)
1 tbsp vegetable oil
1 tbsp grated fresh ginger
2 garlic cloves, crushed
7 oz tofu, drained and cut into cubes
2 green onions, finely sliced

burger with the works

Burger with the works

The hamburger is a legitimate and respectable meal of grilled meat and salad served with bread. It's just served vertically, instead of horizontally. The real key to a good burger is in the build, which is both an art and a science.

SERVES 4
Burgers:
2 slices white bread
½ cup milk
1 lb lean ground beef
1 tbsp minced chives
1 tbsp minced parsley
sea salt
freshly ground black pepper
1 free-range egg, lightly
   beaten
4 slices bacon or pancetta
1 tbsp olive oil

To serve:
4 slices cheese (eg jarlsberg)
4 hamburger buns
4 tbsp tomato relish (see right)
8 lettuce leaves
2 tomatoes, thickly sliced
2 tbsp good mayonnaise

To make the burgers, soak the bread in the milk, squeeze dry, and chop finely. In a bowl, mix the ground beef with the bread, chives, parsley, salt, and pepper. Add the egg, and mix to a mulch with your hands. Form into four thick, bun-sized patties; cover and chill.

Broil or pan-fry the bacon or pancetta until crisp. Heat the olive oil in a heavy-based frying pan and cook the burgers for 3 minutes on each side until well browned. Top each with a cheese slice as it comes off the heat.

Split the buns, and lightly toast the insides only. Top the base bun in this order: tomato relish, lettuce leaves, cheeseburger, bacon, and a slice of tomato. Spread the mayonnaise on the inside lid and place on top.

Tomato relish

Combine 14 oz canned crushed tomatoes, 2 tbsp olive oil, 1 minced onion, 2 crushed garlic cloves, 2 tbsp wine vinegar, and 1 tbsp sugar in a saucepan. Season and cook down until thick and pulpy, stirring occasionally.

Turkey burger

Go beyond the hamburger to the turkey or chicken burger, which is lighter and sweeter. If you find hamburger buns a bit soft and squishy, try lightly toasted English muffins. These are slightly smaller, so it is easier to shape your burger to them.

In a bowl, combine the ground meat, thyme or parsley, bread crumbs, egg, salt, and pepper, and mix with your hands to a mulch. Form the mixture into four balls, then flatten into muffin-sized patties.

If grilling or broiling, brush the patties with the olive oil. If pan-frying, heat the oil in a heavy-based frying pan. Grill, broil, or fry the burgers on both sides until brown and sizzling. This should take around 5 minutes on each side, but check one before serving.

Split the muffins or buns and lightly toast, or toast the insides only. Top each muffin base with a lettuce leaf, cucumber slices, and a burger, adding tomato and avocado slices if you like. Top with cranberry sauce and mayonnaise, and finally the muffin lid.

SERVES 4

Burgers:
1 lb ground turkey or chicken
1 tbsp thyme leaves or chopped parsley
3 tbsp fresh or dry bread crumbs
1 free-range egg, lightly beaten
sea salt
freshly ground black pepper
1 tbsp olive oil

To serve:
4 English muffins or hamburger buns
4 butter lettuce leaves
1/2 hothouse cucumber, peeled and sliced
2 tbsp cranberry sauce
2 tbsp good mayonnaise

Extras:
2 tomatoes, sliced
1/2 avocado, sliced

chicken stir-fry

Chicken stir-fry

The three rules of the stir-fry are: keep it hot, keep it moving, and keep it simple. Flip the food constantly in the wok, and it will stay bright and clear-tasting. It also pays to get everything ready and lined up in order, so nothing is forgotten. (Saves you from that old oops-forgot-to-add-the-chicken syndrome.)

Finely slice the chicken and cut each slice in half. Mix 1 tbsp soy sauce, 1 tbsp rice wine or sherry, and 1 tsp cornstarch together in a bowl. Add the chicken and turn to coat well. Set aside to marinate.

Slice the snow peas lengthwise with the tip of a sharp knife—a bit of an effort but worth it for the effect. Finely slice the celery. Mix the remaining rice wine and cornstarch together and set aside.

Heat a wok until hot. When hot, add the oil and stir-fry the garlic and ginger for 30 seconds. Add the chicken with its marinade, and toss well over high heat for 2 minutes until colored.

Add the snow peas, celery, and bean sprouts, and toss over high heat for 2 minutes. Add the oyster sauce and remaining soy sauce, and toss for 2 minutes. Add the cornstarch mixture and bring to a boil, tossing.

Divide the stir-fry among four deep, warmed bowls and serve with bowls of rice and chopsticks.

SERVES 4

2 skinless, boneless chicken breast halves

3 tbsp soy sauce

2 tbsp Chinese rice wine or dry sherry

2 tsp cornstarch

8 oz snow peas (about 1½ cups)

2 celery stalks

2 tbsp vegetable oil

1 garlic clove, squashed

1 slice fresh ginger, shredded

7 oz bean sprouts (about 2 cups), rinsed

2 tbsp oyster sauce

Chinese spiced beef

A simple, old-fashioned cut of meat cooks itself to tenderness in this classic Chinese braise. I serve it with the garlic, ginger, and whole spices intact, but you can fish them out if you like.

Cut the beef into 1-inch cubes. Heat the oil in a Dutch oven or heavy saucepan and brown the meat lightly, in batches. Return all meat to the pan, add cold water to cover, and bring to a boil, then immediately reduce to a simmer, skimming if necessary.

Stir in the rice wine or sherry, garlic, ginger, green onions, soy sauce, sugar, star anise, and cinnamon sticks. Simmer very gently, partly covered, for 2 hours. Meanwhile, soak the mushrooms in the hot water.

Cut the pumpkin or squash into $^3/_4$-inch cubes, discarding seeds and skin. Drain and halve the mushrooms, discarding stems.

Add the pumpkin cubes and mushrooms to the braise and cook, uncovered, for 30 minutes longer until the beef is tender. Serve in warm bowls, with lots of rice.

SERVES 4

$2^1/_4$lb beef brisket

2 tbsp vegetable oil

3 tbsp Chinese rice wine or dry sherry

2 garlic cloves, bruised

3 thick slices fresh ginger

3 green onions, minced

$^1/_2$ cup soy sauce

3 tbsp brown sugar

4 star anise

4 cinnamon sticks

8 dried Chinese mushrooms

1 cup hot water

1-lb piece of pumpkin or butternut squash

Cavatappi with sausage

Cavatappi is my pasta of the moment, because its corkscrew curls catch and keep all the sauce. And this is my favorite sauce—spicy Italian pork sausage cooked in milk (a grandmotherly trick to make it sweet), and then in tomato. You can't get more comforting than that.

Slit open the sausages and remove the meat, discarding the skins. Finely slice the onion. Heat the olive oil and butter in a frying pan and cook the onion gently for 5 or 6 minutes until soft but not colored.

Add the sausage to the pan in pieces and fry, breaking it up with a wooden spoon, until it is cooked but not browned. Add the milk and simmer very gently, stirring, for 5 minutes until it is all absorbed.

Roughly chop the tomatoes and add them, with their juices, to the pan. Add the sugar, nutmeg, salt, and pepper, and simmer for 15 minutes, stirring occasionally.

In the meantime, cook the pasta in a large pot of boiling salted water until al dente—tender but still firm to the bite.

Add the cream to the sauce and stir, gently heating it through. Drain the pasta, toss well with the sauce, and serve with plenty of grated parmesan.

SERVES 4

6 small, fresh, spicy Italian pork sausages or 3 large ones
1 small onion, peeled
1 tbsp olive oil
1 tbsp butter
$2/3$ cup milk
14 oz canned tomatoes
1 tsp sugar
pinch of freshly grated nutmeg
sea salt
freshly ground black pepper
14 oz cavatappi, penne, or other short tube pasta
2 tbsp cream (optional)
freshly grated parmesan

Beans and wilted arugula

I suspect I spend more on peppery, horseradishy arugula than I do on shoes. I wilt it into pasta, scatter it over risotto and stews, serve it with seafood grills, and generally munch my way through bowls of the stuff. This is a fast way to get lunch on the table.

Heat 2 tbsp olive oil in a saucepan. Add the garlic, tomatoes or purée, sugar, Worcestershire sauce, and mustard, and cook gently for 10 minutes, stirring. Add the beans and parsley, and cook for 5 more minutes, adding a little water if the mixture gets too thick. Season with salt and pepper to taste.

Drop the arugula into a pot of simmering salted water for a few seconds until just wilted, then drain, squeeze out excess water, and chop roughly. Toss in the remaining olive oil, with salt and pepper.

Toast the slices of sourdough bread. Top each slice with the wilted arugula, and spoon the hot beans over the top.

SERVES 6

3 tbsp extra virgin olive oil

2 garlic cloves, crushed

14 oz canned tomatoes, chopped, or 2 cups tomato purée

1 tbsp brown sugar

1 tbsp Worcestershire sauce

1 tsp Dijon mustard

28 oz canned cannellini beans, drained and rinsed

2 tbsp minced parsley

sea salt

freshly ground black pepper

8 oz arugula

4 thick slices sourdough bread

terry's fried egg

Terry's fried egg baguette

My soccer-mad husband has devised a number of different things to eat while watching sports on television. For this simple half-time lunch, he has even developed a brilliant technique for cooking the perfect fried egg.

Heat the 1 tsp olive oil in a nonstick pan. Break in the eggs, cover the pan with a lid, and cook over a very gentle heat for 4 to 5 minutes, depending on the heat, until the whites have set and the yolks have glazed over but are still softly runny.

In the meantime, lightly warm the baguette in the oven for 2 minutes, or split in half and lightly toast the inside surfaces under the broiler.

Halve the cherry tomatoes. Heat 1 tbsp olive oil in a nonstick frying pan. Add the tomatoes and cook for 2 minutes until they soften.

Place the split baguettes on two warm plates and lightly butter if you like. Line each one with ham, place a fried egg on top, and spoon the cherry tomatoes over. Sprinkle with salt and pepper, and serve.

MAKES 2
Terry's fried eggs:
1 tsp olive oil
2 free-range eggs

To serve:
1 fresh baguette
4 cherry tomatoes
1 tbsp olive oil
butter to spread (optional)
2 thin slices good ham
sea salt
freshly ground black pepper

Chorizo and potatoes

Use mild or spicy chorizo sausages from the deli or butcher, and serve this lovely Spanish tapa dish with crusty bread and a glass of red.

Peel the potatoes and cut into roughly ½-inch dice. Cook in simmering salted water for 10 minutes until half-cooked.

Slice the chorizo, and finely slice the onion and celery. Heat half the olive oil in a heavy-based frying pan and sear the chorizo on both sides until browned. Remove the chorizo, then add the remaining oil to the pan and cook the onion and celery for 5 minutes to soften.

Add the potatoes, garlic, sea salt, pepper, and half the paprika; toss well. Add the white wine, bay leaf, and enough water to cover the potatoes. Cook, uncovered, over a medium heat for 10 minutes or until the potatoes are tender.

Return the chorizo to the pan and cook over high heat for a further 5 minutes or until the liquid reduces to a sludgy sauce. Serve warm or at room temperature, sprinkled with the remaining paprika.

SERVES 4

1 lb all-purpose potatoes

salt

2 chorizo sausages

1 onion, peeled

1 celery stalk

2 tbsp olive oil

1 garlic clove, smashed

sea salt

freshly ground black pepper

1 tsp paprika

1 cup dry white wine

1 bay leaf

Stuffed peppers

It's time some of these old-fashioned ideas were brought back into circulation, because they work. Stuff a sweet pepper with meat and rice, and the juices will mingle as the stuffing virtually steams and the pepper cooks, so that the two are one.

Heat the oven to 400°F. Cut the tops off the peppers, retaining them to use as lids. Scoop out the seeds and cut away any major internal ribbing from the insides.

In a bowl, mix the ground meat with the egg, cooked rice, green onions, half the paprika, the parsley, sea salt, and pepper, mulching it with your hands. Add half the tomatoes, mixing well.

Stuff the peppers with the mixture, piling it high. Stand the peppers in a lightly oiled roasting pan and rub the skin with a little of the olive oil. Bake for 1 hour until tender, adding the lightly oiled pepper lids to the pan for the last 15 minutes.

To make the sauce, gently heat the rest of the chopped tomatoes with the remaining olive oil and paprika, the sugar, salt, and pepper.

To serve, place a whole stuffed pepper on each plate, spoon the tomato sauce on and around, and top with the lid.

SERVES 4
2 red bell peppers
2 yellow bell peppers
1 lb ground pork or chicken
1 free-range egg
1 cup cooked rice
4 green onions, minced
1 tsp paprika
1 tbsp minced parsley
sea salt
freshly ground black pepper
14 oz canned crushed tomatoes
2 tbsp olive oil
1 tsp sugar

special

Scallop stack

Beautiful, big scallops may be expensive, but they are worth it. Avoid scallops that have been soaked in water, as these will stew rather than sear, spoiling the dish. To turn this elegant appetizer into a main dish, serve with lemony couscous.

Rinse and dry the scallops. Cut a cross in the base of the tomatoes and dunk them into a pot of boiling water for 20 seconds. Remove and peel. Cut in half, discard the juices and seeds, then cut the flesh into small dice.

Whisk the extra virgin olive oil and lemon juice in a bowl, with sea salt and pepper. Add the diced tomatoes, preserved lemon, and basil or parsley. Toss lightly and set aside.

Heat the olive oil in a heavy-based frying pan and sear the scallops on one side, without moving, for 2 minutes, until crusty. Turn and cook on the other side for less than a minute, until hot in the middle but still moist. Season well.

Stack three scallops on each plate and drizzle with the tomato and lemon vinaigrette to serve.

SERVES 4

12 large scallops, cleaned

2 ripe, red tomatoes

3 tbsp extra virgin olive oil

1 tbsp lemon juice, or more
   to taste

sea salt

freshly ground black pepper

1 tbsp minced preserved lemon

2 tbsp chopped basil or
   flat-leaf parsley

1 tbsp olive oil

Thai seafood soup

"Dtom yam gung" is the most famous of all Thai soups, for its provocative balance of chili, lime juice, and fish sauce. Making the stock from the shrimp heads gives that authentic touch of "red oil" to the broth.

Peel and devein the shrimp, saving heads and shells. Heat the oil in a heavy-based frying pan, add the shrimp heads and shells, and toss well over a fairly high heat, then crush with a potato masher to extract the juices. Add the boiling water and simmer for 10 minutes.

Finely slice the chili pepper and mushrooms. Strain the shrimp stock through a sieve into a saucepan, discarding the heads and shells. Add the lemongrass, chili, mushrooms, and lime leaves, and simmer for 5 minutes. Add the shrimp, sugar, and fish sauce, and simmer for a couple of minutes until the shrimp turn pink.

Remove from the heat, add the lime juice and half the cilantro, and taste for the balance between hot, sweet, and sour flavors. Serve in four deep soup bowls, scattered with the remaining cilantro.

SERVES 4

8 to 12 medium raw shrimp
in shell
1 tbsp vegetable oil
4 cups boiling water
1 small, hot red chili pepper
5 oz button mushrooms or
straw mushrooms
2 lemongrass stalks, white
part only, bashed
4 kaffir lime leaves
1 tbsp sugar
2 tbsp Thai fish sauce
3 tbsp lime juice, or more to
taste
3 tbsp cilantro leaves

Asparagus and pea soup

With any green vegetable soup, I suggest whizzing in a handful of fresh flat-leaf parsley just before serving, to intensify the freshness and the color. Don't feel you have to stand a spear of asparagus in the soup as I did for the photograph here. All cooks have their own ways of amusing themselves, and this was mine.

SERVES 6
2¼lb thick asparagus spears
5 cups chicken stock
1²/₃ cups shelled fresh or
   frozen green peas
sea salt
freshly ground black pepper
handful of flat-leaf parsley
   leaves

Wash the asparagus, then bend the spears until they snap; discard the woody ends. Finely chop the asparagus stalks, reserving the tips for serving.

Bring the chicken stock to a boil, add the chopped asparagus and green peas, and simmer for 15 minutes until soft. Add sea salt and pepper, and taste.

Cool the soup a little, then purée in the blender or food processor in batches. Add the parsley leaves to the last batch.

To serve, gently reheat the soup with the asparagus tips for about 5 minutes, then ladle into four warmed soup bowls. I don't think it needs cream, but you could add a spoonful or two when reheating if you're feeling creamy.

saffron cream mussels

Saffron cream mussels

A touch of saffron and curry powder in the creamy sauce makes these mussels irresistible. Cook the mussels lightly so they are plump, sweet, and still full of their own juices.

Discard any broken mussels, and those that do not close when sharply tapped. Scrub the mussels well and pull out any little "beards." Put the white wine, onion, and garlic in a heavy frying pan, bring to a boil, and boil for 1 minute. Add the mussels, cover tightly, and cook for 1 minute.

Shake the pan and remove any mussels that have opened, then repeat the process, keeping the opened mussels in a covered bowl. Discard any mussels that remain closed. Strain the cooking broth into a glass measuring jug and set aside.

Melt the butter in a small saucepan, sprinkle on the flour, and cook, stirring, for about 3 minutes. Gradually pour in the mussel broth, stirring constantly, then slowly pour in the milk, stirring.

Beat the egg yolk, curry powder, saffron, turmeric, and cream together, then add to the sauce, stirring well; don't let it boil.

Remove the top shells of about half the mussels, and discard. Pile all the mussels into four warmed, shallow bowls and pour the sauce over the top to serve.

SERVES 4

3 lb fresh mussels

1/2 cup dry white wine

1 small onion, minced

1 garlic clove, minced

1 tbsp butter

1 tbsp all-purpose flour

1/2 cup milk

1 egg yolk

1/2 tsp mild curry powder

1/2 tsp powdered saffron

1/2 tsp ground turmeric

1/2 cup heavy cream

Red mullet with laksa sauce

Singaporean laksa is usually a soup with noodles, but I've borrowed the rich, creamy sauce for a special dinner. Keep a jar of curry laksa paste on hand and the sauce is made in 10 minutes. If you can't get red mullet, a member of the goatfish family, try snapper, salmon, sole, or even shrimp instead, or chicken or vegetables. Serve with rice or noodles.

Peel the cucumber and slice it as finely as you can. Salt the cucumber and set aside.

To make the sauce, heat the oil in a frying pan or wok. Add the curry laksa paste and fry for 3 or 4 minutes until fragrant. Add the chicken stock or water, salt, and sugar, and bring to a boil. Reduce to a simmer and add the coconut milk, stirring constantly. Simmer, uncovered, for 5 minutes until lightly creamy.

To cook the fish, heat the oil in a nonstick frying pan and cook the fillets, skin-side down, for 2 to 3 minutes, gently pressing them into the pan to help crisp the skin. Turn and cook the other side for 1 minute. Season with salt and pepper.

Lightly rinse the cucumber and pat dry. Place in the center of four warmed, shallow pasta bowls and top with the red mullet.

Add the lime juice to the hot sauce, and ladle it around the fish. Top with cilantro leaves and serve.

SERVES 4

1 hothouse cucumber
2 tsp fine salt
1 tbsp vegetable oil
4 red mullet or snapper fillets, around 6 oz each
sea salt
freshly ground black pepper
handful of cilantro leaves

Sauce:
1 tbsp vegetable oil
1 tbsp curry laksa paste (eg Reuben Solomon's) or Thai red curry paste
$2/3$ cup chicken stock or water
$1/2$ tsp salt
1 tbsp brown sugar
$1^{3}/4$ cups coconut milk
1 tbsp lime juice

sweet and sour sauce

Sweet and sour fish

If you have been put off sweet-and-sour by the Chinese take-out cliché of glutinous, sickly sweet, crimson sauce, try this sweetly sharp version instead. It is a lot closer to the original Shanghainese recipe, and makes the flavor of the fish jump in your mouth.

SERVES 4

7 oz bean sprouts (about 2 cups)

4 tbsp vegetable oil

4 thick pieces of white fish fillet (eg haddock, cod), around 6 oz each

2 tbsp cornstarch, to coat

2 green onions, finely sliced

Sauce:

6 dried Chinese mushrooms

2-inch piece of fresh ginger

2 tsp cornstarch

3 tbsp rice vinegar or wine vinegar

2 tbsp sugar

2 tbsp tomato ketchup

½ tsp salt

1 tbsp soy sauce

1 tbsp rice wine or dry sherry

1 cup water or chicken stock

Put the dried mushrooms for the sauce in a bowl of boiling water and let soak for 30 minutes. Peel and slice the ginger, then cut into very fine matchsticks.

To make the sauce, drain and finely slice the mushrooms, discarding the stems. Mix the cornstarch and vinegar to a paste. Place in a small saucepan with the sugar, tomato ketchup, salt, soy sauce, rice wine or sherry, water or stock, and mushrooms. Bring to a boil, stirring until the sauce is thick and glossy.

Rinse the bean sprouts and shake dry. Heat half the oil in a frying pan. Add the ginger and fry for 1 minute, stirring, then lift out with a slotted spoon and add to the sauce. Fry the bean sprouts in the pan for 30 seconds, then divide among four warmed dinner plates.

Coat the fish fillets lightly with cornstarch. Heat the remaining oil in the pan and fry the fish fillets for around 3 minutes on each side until golden. Place on the bean sprouts and spoon the hot sauce over. Scatter on the green onions and serve, with rice or noodles.

Salmon, bacon, and peas

Salmon is the little black dress of home entertaining, able to be as formal or casual as you like. Swap the peas for a green salad or grilled vegetables accordingly.

Wrap each salmon fillet in a slice of bacon or pancetta. Mince the rest of the bacon and the onion.

Heat half the olive oil in a frying pan and cook the onion gently for 5 minutes, then add the minced bacon and cook for 10 more minutes until the onion is soft and translucent.

Cook the peas in simmering salted water for 5 minutes or until tender. Drain and refresh under cold running water. Drain well, then add to the bacon and onion with pepper to taste. Reheat gently.

Heat the remaining oil in a nonstick frying pan and sear the salmon for 2 to 3 minutes on each side until the bacon is crisp; the salmon should still be pink in the center. Spoon the peas and bacon onto warmed plates, top with the salmon, and serve.

SERVES 4
4 pieces of salmon fillet,
around 6oz each
8 slices bacon or pancetta
1 onion, peeled
2 tbsp olive oil
3 cups shelled fresh or
frozen green peas
sea salt
freshly ground black pepper

Duck with beets

Duck breasts don't have to be undercooked inside and over-scorched outside. Gently steaming them before pan-frying to crisp and color the skin makes it easy—for both you and the duck—to get it right.

First prepare the beets. Cook the unpeeled beets in boiling water until tender—this can take up to 1 hour, but at least you don't have much to do. Drain, reserving 1 cup of the water. Rinse the beets under cold running water and rub off the skins and stems, then cut into small dice.

Return the beets to the pan. Add the reserved liquid, the vinegar, sugar, salt, and pepper. Bring to a boil, stirring, and let bubble until the liquid is reduced to a slightly sticky syrup. Keep warm.

Meanwhile, wash and dry the duck breasts, and score the skin in a criss-cross pattern using a sharp knife. Rub with the salt and thyme leaves. Place on a heatproof plate that will fit into your steamer and steam over simmering water for 20 minutes. Remove the duck breasts and pat dry. (You can prepare to this stage a few hours ahead.)

Heat the oil in a nonstick frying pan and sear the duck breasts, skin-side down, until the skin is crisp and golden. Turn them over, reduce the heat, and cook gently until heated through.

Carve each duck breast thickly on the diagonal, and serve with the beets and a leafy green salad.

SERVES 4

Beets:

4 medium beets

1/4 cup white vinegar

3/4 cup sugar

1 tsp salt

1/2 tsp freshly ground black pepper

4 duck breast halves with skin, around 7 oz each

1/2 tsp salt

1 tbsp thyme sprigs

2 tsp oil

Rare beef with Thai herbs

The next time you want to "do something special," go and buy a big, beautiful piece of beef. It's an event, a celebration, and, best of all, it rests for an hour before serving so you can do everything in advance. Add a zingy dressing of herbs, chili, fish sauce, and lime juice, and serve it forth to the multitudes.

Place the beef in a shallow dish, rub with the soy sauce and sesame oil, and let marinate for a few hours or overnight.

Heat the oven to 425°F. Heat the vegetable oil in a heavy frying pan and sear the beef until browned and crusty all over.

Transfer the seared beef to a lightly oiled roasting pan and roast for 15 minutes. Reduce the oven setting to 350°F and roast for a further 25 to 30 minutes, for rare to medium rare. Remove and rest the beef under a loose sheet of foil for an hour before carving.

To make the dressing, whisk the lime juice, fish sauce or soy sauce, sesame oil, and sugar together until the sugar has dissolved. Add the shallots, chili pepper, green onions, and herb leaves, and toss well to mix.

Slice the beef, discarding the string, and arrange on a serving platter. Spoon the dressing over the beef and serve, with lime wedges.

SERVES 6 TO 8
2¼-lb beef tenderloin, rolled and tied
2 tbsp soy sauce
1 tbsp toasted sesame oil
2 tbsp vegetable oil
2 limes, quartered

Dressing:
2 tbsp lime juice
2 tbsp Thai fish sauce or soy sauce
1 tbsp toasted sesame oil
2 tsp sugar
4 small shallots, finely sliced
1 small, hot red chili pepper, finely sliced
2 green onions, finely sliced
handful of basil leaves
handful of mint leaves
handful of cilantro leaves

Slashed roast lamb

Lamb slashed almost to the bone cooks faster, remains tender, and looks spectacular. You'll end up with chunky slices coated in a garlicky, lemony seasoning that are a joy to eat. Serve with potatoes roasted in the same pan, and a green salad.

Heat the oven to 425°F. Holding the leg of lamb with its meatiest side toward you, slash 5 times almost to the bone, at 1-inch intervals.

Combine the parsley, garlic, anchovies, capers, lemon zest, and bread crumbs in a bowl. Mix in the olive oil to make a paste. Push between the lamb slashes, reshape the meat, and tie with string.

Scatter with rosemary, drizzle with a little olive oil, and roast for 20 minutes. Reduce the oven to 375°F and continue to roast for 45 minutes to 1 hour. Let rest under foil for 10 minutes.

Strain the juices into a bowl and spoon off surface fat. Remove the string and carve across the lamb, parallel to the bone. Arrange on warm plates, drizzle with the juices, and serve, with lemon wedges.

SERVES 4 TO 6
1 leg of lamb, around 4$\frac{1}{2}$lb
3 tbsp roughly chopped parsley
4 garlic cloves, chopped
2 anchovies, chopped
2 tbsp salted capers, rinsed
1 tbsp coarsely grated
lemon zest
4 tbsp soft fresh bread crumbs
3 tbsp extra virgin olive oil
4 rosemary sprigs
extra olive oil to drizzle
1 lemon, quartered

Cranberry gelatin and cream

This sparkling dessert gelatin is made with easily obtainable cranberry juice. Add a splash of port for a traditional English port wine "jelly."

In a saucepan, combine the cranberry juice, sugar, and port if using. Heat slowly to just under the boil, stirring to dissolve the sugar. Remove the pan from the heat.

Soak the leaf gelatin in cold water for 3 minutes until blobby, then squeeze out the excess water and whisk the gelatin into the hot cranberry liquid until melted. Or sprinkle the granulated gelatin directly over the hot liquid and leave for 1 minute, then whisk well.

SERVES 4

3 cups cranberry juice

½ cup sugar

¼ cup ruby port (optional)

4 gelatin leaves or 2 envelopes granulated gelatin

½ cup light cream

Let cool, stirring occasionally. When cool, pour the cranberry mixture into four 5-oz martini glasses, or four individual molds, and refrigerate until set.

If set in glasses, trickle a little cream over the top of each gelatin until you have a smooth cream "frosting," then serve. If set in molds, turn out onto plates and drizzle with the cream.

162

Berry mascarpone

My lighter, summery version of tiramisu uses strawberries, raspberries, and berry liqueur instead of coffee and cocoa. Like a traditional tiramisu, it goes all cakey, spongey, and creamy, as the flavors swell and ripen.

Halve or quarter the strawberries lengthwise and set aside with the raspberries. In a bowl, beat the eggs and sugar together until creamy, then whisk in the mascarpone until smooth.

Mix the liqueur and milk in a shallow bowl. One at a time, dip half the ladyfingers in the liquid, just long enough to coat, and arrange over the bottom of a large, but not too deep, serving dish.

Cover with a layer of mascarpone cream and scatter with berries. Repeat with another layer of dipped ladyfingers, then mascarpone. Top with a generous layer of berries, letting some sink into the cream. Chill for 4 or 5 hours before serving.

Note: this recipe contains raw egg.

SERVES 6

1 lb strawberries (about 3 cups), hulled

8 oz raspberries (about 2 cups)

3 extra large free-range eggs

1/2 cup sugar

2 cups mascarpone

1/2 cup pink berry liqueur (eg Framboise)

1/2 cup milk

7 oz Italian ladyfingers (savoiardi)

lemon posset

Lemon posset

In medieval England, a posset was a sweetened, lightly curdled milk drink. The modern posset is made from cream and sugar, acidulated with lemon juice. It is just like a rich, gooey lemon curd, without all that mucking around with egg yolks.

Combine the cream and sugar in a saucepan and bring to a boil, stirring. Reduce the heat and bubble for 3 minutes, stirring constantly, without letting the cream boil over.

SERVES 4

2 cups heavy cream

$^2/_3$ cup sugar

$^1/_4$ cup lemon juice

Remove from the heat and add the lemon juice, stirring well. Taste and add a little more lemon juice if you so desire. Let the posset cool for 10 minutes, then stir once more and pour into four 4-oz ramekins, Chinese tea cups, or espresso coffee cups. Cool, then refrigerate for a few hours before serving, with a tiny spoon.

Pineapple vodka crush

This is so spritzy and refreshing that people put a spoonful in their mouth and immediately go "wow." It's great at the end of a barbecue, or after something spicy. And if you put it in the freezer and forget to stir it, don't worry: the vodka prevents it from freezing into a solid block, and after 15 minutes in the refrigerator it will be soft enough to serve.

Cut the top off the pineapple and slice lengthwise into quarters. Slice off and discard the core, then cut the skin and the "eyes" away from the flesh. Cut the pineapple flesh into cubes.

Whiz the pineapple flesh in a blender with the vodka, sugar, lemon juice, and mint leaves.

Pour the mixture into a plastic or other freezerproof container. Freeze for an hour or two until firm on the outside but still liquid in the center. Tip the mixture into a bowl and beat well, then return to the freezer for another hour or so, until partly frozen. Beat again, breaking up any crystals, then freeze until required.

Chill four bowls or glasses. Leave the pineapple crush in the refrigerator for 15 minutes to soften before serving. Scoop into the chilled bowls or glasses and serve, with a sprig of mint on the side.

SERVES 4
1 pineapple, around 2$\frac{1}{4}$lb
$\frac{1}{2}$ cup vodka
$\frac{1}{2}$ cup sugar
1 tbsp lemon juice
15 mint leaves
4 mint sprigs

Frozen chocolate mousse

This is better than ice cream: a rich, creamy, gooey, moussey parfait, ready to slice, chop, or scoop. Use a light hand to fold the cream into the chocolate mixture: better to have a few streaks of cream through the mousse than lose all the lightness and volume.

Melt the chocolate in a heatproof bowl set over a pan of gently simmering water, then set aside to cool for 3 minutes.

In a bowl, beat the eggs, egg yolks, and sugar together for a few minutes, using a hand-held electric mixer, until pale and thick. Add the melted chocolate and beat constantly for about 3 minutes, then stir in the vanilla extract and whisky.

In another bowl, whip the cream until it forms light peaks. Fold the cream lightly through the chocolate, then pour into a 1-quart capacity loaf pan. Cover with plastic wrap and freeze overnight.

To serve, soften the mousse in the refrigerator for 15 minutes, or dip the base of the pan very briefly in hot water and run a knife around the edges. Unmold and cut into thick slices or chunks, or scoop straight from the pan. Serve immediately, dusted with cocoa powder.

Note: this recipe contains raw egg.

SERVES 6

7oz dark, bittersweet
  chocolate, chopped
2 extra large free-range eggs,
  plus 2 egg yolks
1/2 cup sugar
1 tsp vanilla extract
2 tbsp Scotch whisky, Cognac,
  or Amaretto liqueur
1 cup heavy cream
unsweetened cocoa powder,
  to dust

Simple passion fruit soufflé

Even the biggest scaredy cat can now make a soufflé. This is based on the lightest, tangiest, most beautiful soufflé in the world, that of the revered (and retired) Fredy Girardet of Switzerland. There are no sauces to make and no sorcery to employ—just egg yolks and whites, passion fruit, and sugar.

Heat the oven to 400°F. Butter the insides of four small individual soufflé dishes or ramekins, lightly dust each one with 1 tsp superfine sugar, tipping out any excess, and place on a baking sheet.

Strain the passion fruit pulp until you have 4 tbsp juice; discard the seeds. In a bowl, beat the egg yolks with ⅓ cup superfine sugar until pale and smooth. Add the passion fruit juice, beating well.

SERVES 4

1 tbsp melted butter

½ cup superfine sugar, plus 4 tsp for the dishes

½ cup passion fruit pulp (about 4 passion fruit)

3 free-range eggs, separated, plus 2 egg whites

confectioners' sugar, to dust

Whisk the 5 egg whites in a large, clean bowl. Add half of the remaining superfine sugar and whisk until they start to thicken. Add the remaining superfine sugar and keep whisking until soft peaks form. Gently fold one-third of the egg whites into the yolks, then fold in the remainder.

Fill the soufflé dishes to the brim and smooth the tops. Bake just below the middle of the oven for 10 minutes until puffed and golden.

Dust each soufflé with confectioners' sugar, gently place on a serving plate, and serve immediately, with cream or ice cream to one side.

Note: if superfine sugar is unavailable use ordinary sugar and process in a food processor for a minute or two.

Lemon sugar crêpes

When I was a child, Italian restaurants served a magical dish of hot golden crêpes with lemon juice and sugar.

Blend the flour, sugar, salt, melted butter, whole egg, and egg yolk in the food processor. Add the milk gradually, with the motor running, to make a smooth and creamy batter. Let rest for at least 30 minutes.

Brush a crêpe pan or small nonstick frying pan with melted butter and place on a medium heat. When hot, add a ladleful of batter and swirl the pan so the batter covers the bottom thinly. Cook for a minute or two until the base of the crêpe is lightly golden.

Turn the crêpe over and cook the other side very briefly. Slide onto a warm plate, sprinkle with sugar, and roll into a tight cigar-like cylinder. Cover and keep warm while you do the rest.

Serve two crepês per person on warm plates, sprinkled with extra sugar and lemon juice. Serve with ice cream and a wedge of lemon.

MAKES 8
Batter:
$^2/_3$ cup all-purpose flour
3 tbsp sugar
pinch of salt
1 tbsp melted butter
1 free-range egg, plus
1 egg yolk
7 fl oz milk
extra melted butter to cook

To serve:
2 tbsp sugar
juice of 2 lemons
1 lemon, quartered

173

fruit

Warm spiced cherries Make a syrup by heating $^1/_2$ cup sugar with 1 cup water, a squeeze of lemon juice, and 4 cloves. Add $2^1/_2$ cups pitted ripe cherries and gently poach for 2 minutes. Add 2 tbsp cherry or berry liqueur and serve warm with thick cream or a wedge of chocolate cake.

Spicy saffron pears Peel 4 ripe, firm pears and poach in a syrup made by heating $^1/_2$ cup sugar with a large pinch of saffron, a few cardamom pods, and enough dry white wine to cover. Serve with a dollop of yogurt and a grind of black pepper.

Caramel apples Peel, quarter, and core 4 apples and sizzle in a nonstick frying pan with 2 tbsp butter, 2 tbsp brown sugar, and 2 tbsp golden raisins until golden. Serve with ice cream or crème fraîche.

Peach and prosciutto Serve a perfect fresh peach with a platter of thinly sliced prosciutto, a wedge of lemon, and a generous arugula and parmesan salad for a summer lunch. Or cut the peach into segments and wrap each in a short length of prosciutto for nibbles with drinks.

Vineyard sausages Slowly sizzle some garlicky fresh pork sausages in a pan, then add a handful of green grapes. Cook until the grapes warm, split, and spill their juices into the pan. Serve the sausages on an arugula salad with the grapey juices spooned over.

Red berry wine Press a pint of fresh berries through a fine sieve, and stir the juices into 4 glasses of well-chilled dessert wine. Add a dash of Cointreau or berry liqueur to sweeten if it tastes too tart.

Red berry meringues Crush two-thirds of a pint of raspberries with a fork, then gently mix with the remaining whole berries. Sandwich 16 crisp little meringues together with whipped cream and the berries for a dessert or afternoon tea.

Toffee-lime bananas Cut 4 unpeeled bananas in half lengthwise. Sprinkle the cut sides with 4 tsp sugar and place under the broiler until the sugar bubbles and browns. Serve the soft bananas with chilled crème fraîche, sour cream, or ice cream and a lime wedge.

Balsamic strawberrries Wash 1 lb strawberries (about 3 cups) and hull. Place in a bowl with 2 tbsp balsamic vinegar and a grind of black pepper, toss lightly, and leave for an hour before serving. The vinegar and pepper intensify the flavor and tend to disappear into the berries.

Berry swizzlers Thread blueberries, strawberries, and raspberries on little bamboo skewers. Dust with confectioners' sugar and serve as a chic dessert with yogurt for dipping, or use as a swizzle stick in cocktails, fruit punches, and fresh fruit smoothies.

Frosted grapes A pretty way to finish a cake, fruit tart, or gelatin dessert. Frost little bunches of 3 or 4 grapes, by painting the grapes with lightly whisked egg white and gently rolling them in sugar.

Sunday roast fruit When you next roast a leg of pork or a duck, cut 4 mandarin oranges or clementines in half and add them to the roasting juices for the last 30 minutes. Serve warm, ready to squeeze over the meat for an instant citrus sauce.

red berry meringues

chocolate pear pudding

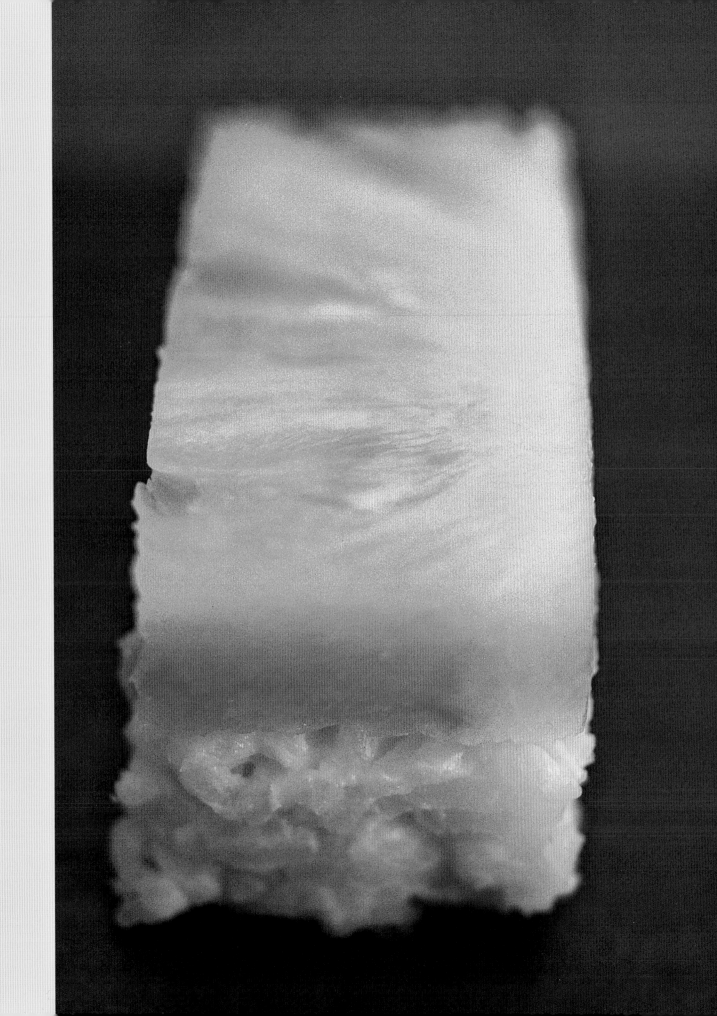

Chocolate pear pudding

I like these two-for-the-price-of-one desserts. In this lush, gooey chocolate pudding, you also get tender baked pears peeking out. If your pears are slightly under-ripe, first poach them in white wine and sugar for 10 minutes.

Heat the oven to 325°F. Beat the butter and sugar together in a bowl until smooth. Add the eggs, one at a time, beating well.

Sift the flour, cocoa powder, and baking powder together over the mixture and beat well with a wooden spoon. Add the milk, stirring until smooth. Spoon the mixture into a lightly buttered 12- x 8-inch baking or gratin dish and spread evenly.

Peel the pears and cut a $\frac{1}{2}$-inch slice from the base of each one so they will stand upright. Push them firmly into the chocolate batter.

Bake for 30 minutes or until the pudding has puffed up around the pears and set at the edges, but is still a bit gooey in the center. Serve with cream or crème fraîche.

SERVES 4

9 tbsp ($4\frac{1}{2}$ oz) butter, melted

1 cup sugar

3 extra large free-range eggs

$1\frac{1}{4}$ cups all-purpose flour

$\frac{3}{4}$ cup unsweetened cocoa
   powder

1 tsp baking powder

5 tbsp milk

4 ripe pears

Pineapple sushi

No, not sushi as in raw fish, but sushi as in sweet coconut rice topped with fresh tangy pineapple. Fresh mango works beautifully, too. You can pick the sushi up and eat them in your fingers, or serve with a dessert knife and fork.

Put the rice, sugar, coconut milk, and water in a saucepan, and bring to a boil, stirring constantly to prevent sticking. Simmer very gently, uncovered, on the lowest possible heat for 20 minutes; stir occasionally, and keep an eye on it to avoid any boiling over.

Once the rice has absorbed the liquid but is not yet cooked, cover the pan tightly and leave over the same gentle heat for 10 more minutes until the rice is tender.

Lightly rinse out an 8- x 6-inch shallow pan or baking dish. Tip in the rice and spread it out evenly, to a $^3/_4$-inch depth. Smooth the top and let cool. Cover with plastic wrap and chill for an hour or two.

When chilled, cut the rice into fingers, each about $1^1/_4$ x 3 inches. Trim the pineapple flesh into matching oblongs, and place on top. Serve one or two sushi fingers per person.

MAKES 12
$1^1/_2$ cups sushi rice
$^1/_2$ cup sugar
1 cup canned coconut milk
$1^3/_4$ cups water
1 lb peeled, cored fresh
pineapple

Banana bread

This cake-like banana bread will stay moist for several days of breakfasts, brunches, afternoon teas, and I'll-just-have-a-small-slice-before-bed moments.

Heat the oven to 350°F. Lightly butter a $8\frac{1}{2}$- x $4\frac{1}{2}$-inch loaf pan. Sift the flour, baking powder, and salt into a bowl; set aside. Mash the bananas to a purée.

Cream the butter and sugar together in a bowl, with a hand-held electric mixer, until smooth and pale. Add the eggs one at a time, beating well until just combined.

Fold in the mashed bananas, vanilla, and walnuts, using a spatula, then lightly fold in the flour. Spoon the batter into the loaf pan.

Bake for 1 hour or until a skewer inserted in the middle comes out dry, covering the top with foil if it starts to brown too quickly. Let cool in the pan for 20 minutes before unmolding. Serve warm or at room temperature, cut into thick slices.

SERVES 8

$1\frac{2}{3}$ cups all-purpose flour

2 tsp baking powder

pinch of salt

3 ripe bananas, around 1 lb

9 tbsp ($4\frac{1}{2}$ oz) butter, softened

$\frac{3}{4}$ cup sugar

2 extra large free-range eggs

$\frac{1}{2}$ tsp vanilla extract

$\frac{1}{2}$ cup chopped walnuts

Little berry cakes

To do these as chic little petits fours, you will need a mini muffin pan or petits four pan. Otherwise, call them not-so-little berry cakes and bake them in a standard muffin pan.

Heat the oven to 325°F. Lightly butter a 24-hole mini muffin pan (or a 12-hole muffin pan) or line with muffin paper liners.

Using an electric mixer, beat the softened butter and granulated sugar together until smooth. Beat in the eggs, one at a time. Sift in the flour, baking powder and salt, and fold through until well mixed. Finally, stir in the milk and vanilla until smooth.

Spoon the batter into the muffin cups. Drop a single berry on top of each little cake (place three on larger cakes).

Bake little cakes for 12 to 15 minutes, larger ones for 18 to 20 minutes, or until a skewer inserted in the center comes out clean.

Let cool to room temperature, then dust with confectioners' sugar and serve.

MAKES 12 OR 24
9 tbsp (4$\frac{1}{2}$oz) butter, softened
$\frac{1}{2}$ cup plus 2 tbsp granulated sugar
3 extra large free-range eggs
1$\frac{1}{4}$ cups all-purpose flour
2 tsp baking powder
pinch of salt
$\frac{1}{4}$ cup milk
$\frac{1}{2}$ tsp vanilla extract
24 or 36 raspberries or blueberries
confectioners' sugar to dust

Chocolate cup cakes

Cakes made with cocoa powder are lighter than those made with chocolate. I take this to mean you can eat more of them.

Heat the oven to 350°F. Line the cups of a 12-hole muffin pan with muffin paper liners.

Using an electric mixer, beat the softened butter and granulated sugar until smooth. Beat in the eggs, one at a time. Sift in the flour, baking powder and cocoa powder, and fold through until well mixed.

Spoon the batter into the muffin cups and bake for 15 to 20 minutes until the tops spring back to the touch. Leave in the muffin pan for 5 minutes, then transfer to a wire rack to cool completely.

Dust the cup cakes with confectioners' sugar. Or, to make the icing, melt the chocolate and butter in a heatproof bowl set over simmering water, stir until smooth, and let cool for 5 to 10 minutes to thicken. Spread each cup cake with icing and sprinkle with gold leaf, then let set.

MAKES 12
11 tbsp (5$\frac{1}{2}$oz) butter, softened
1 cup granulated sugar
4 extra large free-range eggs
1 cup all-purpose flour
1$\frac{1}{2}$tsp baking powder
$\frac{1}{2}$ cup unsweetened cocoa powder
confectioners' sugar to dust

Chocolate icing:
2oz dark, bittersweet chocolate, chopped
4 tbsp butter
edible gold leaf sprinkles (from cake decorating specialists)

recipe index

index

conversions

volume

1 ml	$^1/_4$ teaspoon
2.5 ml	$^1/_2$ teaspoon
5 ml	1 teaspoon
7.5 ml	$1^1/_2$ teaspoons
10 ml	2 teaspoons
15 ml	1 tablespoon
30 ml	2 tablespoons / 1 fl oz
60 ml	$^1/_4$ cup / 2 fl oz
80 ml	$^1/_3$ cup
120 ml	$^1/_2$ cup / 4 fl oz
160 ml	$^2/_3$ cup
180 ml	$^3/_4$ cup / 6 fl oz
240–250 ml	1 cup / 8 fl oz
300 ml	$1^1/_4$ cups / 10 fl oz
360 ml	$1^1/_2$ cups / 12 fl oz
420 ml	$1^3/_4$ cups / 14 fl oz
480–500 ml	2 cups / 1 pint / 16 fl oz
720–750 ml	3 cups / 24 fl oz
.95–1 liter	4 cups / 1 quart / 32 fl oz
1 liter	1.06 quarts
3.8 liters	4 quarts / 1 gallon

weight

7 g	$^1/_4$ oz
15 g	$^1/_2$ oz
20 g	$^3/_4$ oz
30 g	1 oz
40 g	$1^1/_2$ oz
55 g	2 oz
65 g	$2^1/_4$ oz
70 g	$2^1/_2$ oz
80 g	$2^3/_4$ oz
85 g	3 oz
90 g	$3^1/_2$ oz
115 g	4 oz
125 g	$4^1/_2$ oz
140 g	5 oz
150 g	6 oz
200 g	7 oz
225 g	8 oz
255 g	9 oz
285 g	10 oz
310 g	11 oz
340 g	12 oz
370 g	13 oz
400 g	14 oz
425 g	15 oz
455 g	1 lb
500 g	1 lb 2 oz
565 g	$1^1/_4$ lb
600 g	1 lb 5 oz
680 g	$1^1/_2$ lb
700 g	1 lb 9 oz
750 g	1 lb 10 oz
800 g	$1^3/_4$ lb
905 g	2 lb
1 kg	2 lb 3 oz

length

5 mm	$^1/_4$ inch
1 cm	$^1/_2$ inch
2.5 cm	1 inch
5 cm	2 inches
7.5 cm	3 inches
10 cm	4 inches
12 cm	5 inches
15 cm	6 inches
18 cm	7 inches
20 cm	8 inches
23 cm	9 inches
25 cm	10 inches
28 cm	11 inches
30 cm	12 inches

oven temperatures

140°C	275°F	Very low
150°C	300°F	Low
170°C	325°F	Moderately low
180°C	350°F	Moderate
200°C	400°F	Hot
220°C	425°F	Hot
230°C	450°F	Very hot